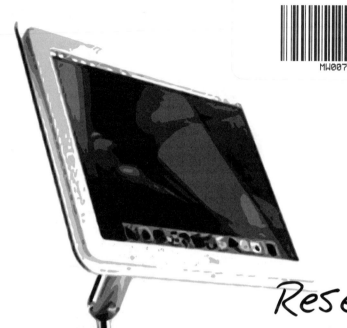

Research Navigator.com Guide: The Helping Professions

Joanne Yaffe
University of Utah

Linda R. Barr
University of the Virgin Islands

PEARSON

Boston | New York | San Francisco
Mexico City | Montreal | Toronto | London | Madrid | Munich | Paris
Hong Kong | Singapore | Tokyo | Cape Town | Sydney

MW00717143

ISBN   0-205-51699-8

Printed in the United States of America

10 9 8 7 6 5 4 3 2 1   11 10 09 08 07 06

Contents

Introduction

Your professor assigns a ten-page research paper that's due in two weeks—and you need to make sure you have up-to-date, credible information. Where do you begin? Today, the easiest answer is the Internet—because it can be so convenient and there is so much information out there. But therein lies part of the problem. How do you know if the information is reliable and from a trustworthy source?

ResearchNavigator.com Guide is designed to help you select and evaluate research from the Web to help you find the best and most credible information you can. Throughout this guide, you'll find:

- **A practical and to-the-point discussion of search engines.** Find out which search engines are likely to get you the information you want and how to phrase your searches for the most effective results.
- **Detailed information on evaluating online sources.** Locate credible information on the Web and get tips for thinking critically about Web sites.
- **Citation guidelines for Web resources.** Learn the proper citation guidelines for Web sites, email messages, listservs, and more.
- **ResearchNavigator.com Guide.** All you need to know to get started with ResearchNavigator.com, a research database that gives you immediate access to hundreds of scholarly journals and other popular publications, such as *Scientific American, U.S. News & World Report,* and many others.

So before running straight to your browser, take the time to read through this copy of *ResearchNavigator.com Guide* and use it as a reference for all of your Web research needs.

P A R T **1**

Research Navigator.com

What Is ResearchNavigator.com?

ResearchNavigator.com is the easiest way for you to start a research assignment or research paper. Complete with extensive help on the research process and four exclusive databases of credible and reliable source material (including EBSCO's ContentSelect™ Academic Journal and Abstract Database, *New York Times* Search by Subject Archive, Link Library, and the *Financial Times* Article Archive), ResearchNavigator.com helps you quickly and efficiently make the most of your research time.

ResearchNavigator.com includes four databases of dependable source material to get your research process started:

1. EBSCO's ContentSelect™ Academic Journal and Abstract Database, organized by subject, contains 50–100 of the leading academic journals per discipline. Instructors and students can search the online journals by keyword, topic, or multiple topics. Articles include abstract and citation information and can be cut, pasted, emailed, or saved for later use.

2. The *New York Times* Search by Subject Archive is organized by academic subject and searchable by keyword, or multiple keywords. Instructors and students can view full-text articles from the world's leading journalists from *The New York Times.* The *New York Times* Search by Subject Archive is available exclusively to instructors and students through ResearchNavigator.com.

3. Link Library, organized by subject, offers editorially selected "Best of the Web" sites. Link libraries are continually scanned and kept up to date, providing the most relevant and accurate links for research assignments.

4. The *Financial Times* Article Archive and Company Financials provides a searchable one-year archive and five-year financials for the 500 largest U.S. companies (by gross revenue).

In addition, ResearchNavigator.com includes extensive online content detailing the steps in the research process including:

- Understanding the Research Process
- Finding Sources for your Assignment
- Using your Library for Research, with library guides to 31 core disciplines. Each library guide includes an overview of major databases and online journals, key associations and newsgroups, and suggestions for further research.
- Writing Your Research Assignment
- Finishing with Endnotes and a Bibliography

Registering with ResearchNavigator.com

http://www.researchnavigator.com

ResearchNavigator.com is simple to use and easy to navigate. The goal of ResearchNavigator.com is to help you complete research assignments or research papers quickly and efficiently. The site is organized around the following five tabs:

- The Research Process
- Finding Sources
- Using Your Library
- Start Writing
- Endnotes & Bibliography

In order to begin using ResearchNavigator.com, you must first register using the personal access code that appears in the front cover of this book.

To Register:
4. Go to **http://www.researchnavigator.com**
5. Click "Register" under "New Users" on the left side of the screen.
6. Enter the access code exactly as it appears on the inside front cover of this book. (Note: Access codes can only be used once to com-

plete one registration. If you purchased a used guide, the access code may not work. Please go to **www.researchnavigator.com** for information on how to obtain a new access code.)

7. Follow the instructions on screen to complete your registration—you may click the Help button at any time if you are unsure how to respond.

8. Once you have successfully completed registration, write down the Login Name and Password you just created and keep it in a safe place. You will need to enter it each time you want to revisit ResearchNavigator.com.

9. Once you register, you have access to all the resources in ResearchNavigator.com for twelve months.

Getting Started

From the ResearchNavigator.com homepage, you have easy access to all of the site's main features, including a quick route to four exclusive databases of source content that will be discussed in greater detail on the following pages. If you are new to the research process, you may want to start by clicking the *Research Process* tab, located in the upper right hand section of the page. Here you will find extensive help on all aspects of the research process, including:

- Overview of the Research Process
- Understanding a Research Assignment
- Finding a Topic
- Creating Effective Notes
- Research Paper Paradigms
- Understanding and Finding "Source" Material
- Understanding and Avoiding Plagiarism
- Summary of the Research Process

For those of you who are already familiar with the research process, you already know that the first step in completing a research assignment or research paper is to select a topic. (In some cases, your instructor may assign you a topic.) According to James D. Lester in *Writing Research Papers,* choosing a topic for the research paper can be easy (any topic will serve) yet very complicated (an informed choice is critical). He suggests selecting a person, a person's work, or a specific issue to study—President George W. Bush, John Steinbeck's *Of Mice and Men,* or learned dexterity with Nintendo games. Try to select a topic that will meet three demands.

1. It must examine a significant issue.
2. It must address a knowledgeable reader and carry that reader to another level of knowledge.

3. It must have a serious purpose, one that demands analysis of the issues, argues from a position, and explains complex details.

You can find more tips from Lester in the *Research Process* section of ResearchNavigator.com.

ResearchNavigator.com simplifies your research efforts by giving you a convenient launching pad for gathering data on your topic. The site has aggregated four distinct types of source material commonly used in research assignments: academic journals (Content-Select™); newspaper articles (*New York Times*), World Wide Web sites (Link Library), and international news and business data (*Financial Times*).

EBSCO's ContentSelect Academic Journal and Abstract Database

EBSCO's ContentSelect Academic Journal and Abstract Database contains scholarly, peer-reviewed journals (like the *Journal of Clinical Psychology* or the *Journal of Anthropology*). A scholarly journal is an edited collection of articles written by various authors and is published several times per year. All the issues published in one calendar year comprise a volume of that journal. For example, the *American Sociological Review* published volume 65 in the year 2000. This official journal of the American Sociological Association is published six times a year, so issues 1–6 in volume 65 are the individual issues for that year. Each issue contains between 4 and 8 articles written by a variety of authors. Additionally, journal issues may contain letters from the editor, book reviews, and comments from authors. Each issue of a journal does not necessarily revolve around a common theme. In fact, most issues contain articles on many different topics.

Scholarly journals, are similar to magazines in that they are published several times per year and contain a variety of articles in each issue, however, they are NOT magazines. What sets them apart from popular magazines like *Newsweek* or *Science News* is that the content of each issue is peer-reviewed. This means that each journal has, in addition to an editor and editorial staff, a pool of reviewers. Rather than a staff of writers who write something on assignment, journals accept submissions from academic researchers all over the world. The editor relies on these peer reviewers both to evaluate the articles, which are submitted, and to decide if they should be accepted for publication. These published articles provide you with a specialized knowledge and information about your research topic. Academic journal articles adhere to strict scientific guidelines for methodology and theoretical grounding. The information obtained in these individual articles is more scientific than information you would find in a popular magazine, newspaper article, or on a Web page.

Using ContentSelect

Searching for articles in ContentSelect is easy! Here are some instructions and search tips to help you find articles for your research paper.

Select a Database

ContentSelect's homepage features a list of databases. To search within a single database, click the name of the database. To search in more than one database, hold down the alt or command key while clicking on the name of the database.

Basic Search. After selecting one or more databases, you must enter a keyword or keywords, then click on "go." This will take you to the basic search window. If you've selected a precise and distinctive keyword, your search may be done. But if you have too many results—which is often the case—you need to narrow your search.

Standard Search (Boolean).
- **AND** combines search terms so that each result contains all of the terms. For example, search **education AND technology** to find only articles that contain both terms.
- **OR** combines search terms so that each result contains at least one of the terms. For example, search **education OR technology** to find results that contain either term.
- **NOT** excludes terms so that each result does not contain the term that follows the "not" operator. For example, search **education NOT technology** to find results that contain the term education but not the term technology.

Search by Article Number. Each and every article in the EBSCO ContentSelect Academic Journal and Abstract Database is assigned its own unique article number. In some cases, you may know the exact article number for the journal article you'd like to retrieve. Perhaps you noted it during a prior research session on ResearchNavigator.com. Such article numbers might also be found on a companion web site for your text, or in the text itself.

To retrieve a specific article, simply type that article number in the "Search by Article Number" field and click the **GO** button.

Advanced Search.   On the tabbed tool bar, click **Advanced Search.** The advanced search window appears. Enter your search terms in the **Find** field. Your search terms can be keywords or selections from search history. Boolean operators (AND, OR, NOT) can also be included in your search.

You can also use **field codes** with your search terms. Fields refer to searchable aspects of an article or Web page; in the case of ContentSelect, they include author, title, subject, abstract, and journal name. Click **Field Codes** to display a list of field codes available with the databases you are using. Type the field code before your search terms to limit those words to the field you entered. For example, **AU Naughton** will find records that contain Naughton in the author field.

To **print, e-mail, or save** several search results, click on the folder next to the result; then print, e-mail, or save from the folder at the top of the results field. (You can still print, e-mail, or save individual results from the open article or citation.)

You can remove specific results, or clear the entire folder and collect new results, during your session. If you end your session, or it times out due to inactivity, the folder is automatically cleared.

Full-Text Results.   Some ContentSelect results will be available in full text—that is, if you click on the full text logo at the bottom of an entry, you will be able to call up the entire journal or magazine article. If you want to limit your search to results available in full text, click on the "search options" tab, and then on "full text." Then renew your search.

Abstract and Citation Results.   Many ContentSelect results are in the form of citations containing abstracts. A **citation** is a bibliographic reference to an article or document, with basic information such as ISSN (International Standard Serial Number, the standard method for identifying publications) and publisher that will help you locate it. An **abstract** is a brief description of an article, usually written by the author. An abstract will help you decide whether you want to locate the work—either in an electronic database or a print version—through your college library.

A handy tip: once you have found an article that meets your research needs, you can search fields easily from the article citation to turn up similar articles. For example, suppose a particular 2005 story from the *Christian Science Monitor* suits your paper perfectly. Go to the citation and click on the subject field to find similar articles. Or, if you want to see what else the author has written, click on the author field to produce a list of articles he or she has written.

In many cases you can search the full text of articles using electronic databases and then read the entire article online. Typically, in order to use these databases you need to have a library card number or special password provided by the library. But sometimes when you use an electronic database you will find that the text of an article won't be accessible online, so you'll have to go to the library's shelves to find the magazine or newspaper in which the article originally appeared.

The *New York Times* Search by Subject Archive

Newspapers, also known as periodicals because they are issued in periodic installments (e.g., daily, weekly, or monthly), provide contemporary information. Information in periodicals—journals, magazines, and newspapers—may be useful, or even critical, when you are ready to focus in on specific aspects of your topic, or to find more up-to-date information.

There are some significant differences between newspaper articles and journal articles, and you should consider the level of scholarship that is most appropriate for your research. Popular or controversial topics may not be well covered in journals, even though coverage in newspapers and "general interest" magazines like *Newsweek* and *Science* for that same topic may be extensive.

ResearchNavigator.com gives you access to a one-year, "search by subject" archive of articles from one of the world's leading newspapers—*The New York Times.* To learn more about *The New York Times,* visit them on the Web at **http://www.nytimes.com**.

Using the search-by-subject archive is easy. Simply select a subject and type a word, or multiple words separated by commas, into the search box and click "go." The *New York Times* search by subject archive sorts article results by relevance, with the most relevant appearing first. To view the most recently published articles first, use the "Sort by" pull-down menu located just above the search results. You can further refine your search as needed. Articles can be printed or saved for later use in your research assignment. Be sure to review the citation rules for how to cite a newspaper article in endnotes or a bibliography.

"Best of the Web" Link Library

The third database included on ResearchNavigator.com, Link Library, is a collection of Web links, organized by academic subject and key terms. To use this database, simply select an academic subject from the dropdown list, and then find the key term for the topic you are searching. Click on the key term and see a list of five to seven editorially reviewed Web sites that offer educationally relevant and reliable content. For example, if your research topic is "Allergies," you may want to select the academic subject Biology and then click on "Allergies" for links to web sites that explore this topic. Simply click on the alphabet bar to view other key terms in Biology, and their corresponding links. The web links in Link Library are monitored and updated each week, reducing your incidence of finding "dead" links.

International *Financial Times* Article Archive

ResearchNavigator.com's fourth database of content is the *Financial Times* Article Archive and Company Financials Database. Through an exclusive agreement with the *Financial Times,* a leading daily newspaper covering national and international news and business, you can search this publication's one-year archive for news stories affecting countries, companies, and people throughout the world. Simply enter your keyword(s) in the text box and click the **GO** button.

Using Your Library

After you have selected your topic and gathered source material from the three databases of content on ResearchNavigator.com, you may need to complete your research by going to your school library. ResearchNavigator.com does not try to replace the library, but rather helps you understand how to use library resources effectively and efficiently.

You may put off going to the library to complete research assignments or research papers because the library can seem overwhelming. ResearchNavigator.com provides a bridge to the library by taking you through a simple step-by-step overview of how to make the most of your library time. Written by a library scientist, the *Using Your Library* tab explains:

- Major types of libraries
- What the library has to offer
- How to choose the right library tools for a project
- The research process
- How to make the most of research time in the library

In addition, when you are ready to use the library to complete a research assignment or research paper, ResearchNavigator.com includes 31 discipline-specific "library guides" for you to use as a roadmap. Each guide includes an overview of the discipline's major subject databases, online journals, and key associations and newsgroups.

For more information and detailed walk-throughs, please visit
www.researchnavigator.com/about

Start Writing

Once you've become well acquainted with the steps in the research process and gathered source materials from ResearchNavigator.com and your school library, it's time to begin writing your assignment. Content found in this tab will help you do just that, beginning with a discussion on how to draft a research paper in an academic style. Other areas addressed include:

- Blending reference material into your writing
- Writing the introduction, body, and conclusion
- Revising, proofreading, and formatting the rough draft
- Online *Grammar Guide* that spells out some of the rules and conventions of standard written English. Included are guidelines and examples for good sentence structure; tips for proper use of articles, plurals and possessives, pronouns, adjectives and adverbs; details on subject-verb agreement and verb tense consistency; and help with the various forms of punctuation.

This is also the tab where you will find sample research papers for your reference. Use them as a guide to writing your own assignment.

Endnotes & Bibliography

The final step in a research assignment is to create endnotes and a bibliography. In an era dubbed "The Information Age," knowledge and words are taking on more significance than ever. Laws requiring writers to document or give credit to the sources of information, while evolving, must be followed.

Various organizations have developed style manuals detailing how to document sources in their particular disciplines. For writing in the humanities and social sciences, the Modern Language Association (MLA) and American Psychological Association (APA) guidelines are the most commonly used, but others, such as those in *The Chicago Manual of Style* (CMS), are also required. The purpose of this Research Navigator™ tab is to help you properly cite your research sources. It contains detailed information on MLA, APA, CMS, and CBE styles. You'll also find guidance on how to cite the material you've gathered right from ResearchNavigator.com!

This Research Navigator tab also provides students with the option to use **AutoCite.** Students just select their documentation style (MLA or APA), and then fill in the fields with information about their source. **AutoCite** will do the rest! It will automatically create the entry in the proper format. Once completed, **AutoCite** will also generate a "Works Cited" or "References" list that students can print or save (cut and paste).

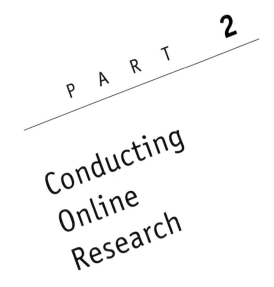

P A R T **2**

Conducting Online Research

Finding Sources:
Search Engines and Subject Directories

Your professor has just given you an assignment to give a five minute speech on the topic "gun control." After a (hopefully brief) panic attack, you begin to think of what type of information you need before you can write the speech. To provide an interesting introduction, you decide to involve your class by taking a straw poll of their views for and against gun control, and to follow this up by giving some statistics on how many Americans favor (and oppose) gun control legislation and then by outlining the arguments on both sides of the issue. If you already know the correct URL for an authoritative Web site like Gallup Opinion Polls (www.gallup.com) or other sites you are in great shape! However, what do you do when you don't have a clue as to which Web site would have information on your topic? In these cases, many, many people routinely (and mistakenly) go to Yahoo! and type in a single term (e.g., guns). This approach is sure to bring first a smile to your face when the results offer you 200,874 hits on your topic, but just as quickly make you grind your teeth in frustration when you start scrolling down the hit list and find sites that range from gun dealerships, to reviews of the video "Young Guns," to aging fan sites for "Guns and Roses."

Finding information on a specific topic on the Web is a challenge. The more intricate your research need, the more difficult it is to find the one or two Web sites among the billions that feature the information you want. This section is designed to help you to avoid frustration and to focus in on the right site for your research by using search engines, subject directories, and meta-sites.

Search Engines

Search engines (sometimes called search services) are becoming more numerous on the Web. Originally, they were designed to help users search the Web by topic. More recently, search engines have added features which enhance their usefulness, such as searching a particular part of the Web (e.g., only sites of educational institutions— dot.edu), retrieving just one site which the search engine touts as most relevant (like Ask.com {www.ask.com}), or retrieving up to 10 sites which the search engine rank as most relevant (like Google {www.google.com}).

Search Engine Defined

According to Cohen (1999):

> "A search engine service provides a searchable database of Internet files collected by a computer program called a wanderer, crawler, robot, worm, or spider. Indexing is created from the collected files, and the results are presented in a schematic order. There are no selection criteria for the collection of files.
>
> A search service therefore consists of three components: (1) a spider, a program that traverses the Web from link to link, identifying and reading pages; (2) an index, a database containing a copy of each Web page gathered by the spider; and (3) a search engine mechanism, software that enables users to query the index and then returns results in a schematic order (p. 31)."

One problem students often have in their use of search engines is that they are deceptively easy to use. Like our example "guns," no matter what is typed into the handy box at the top, links to numerous Web sites appear instantaneously, lulling students into a false sense of security. Since so much was retrieved, surely SOME of it must be useful. WRONG! Many Web sites retrieved will be very light on substantive content, which is not what you need for most academic endeavors. Finding just the right Web site has been likened to finding diamonds in the desert.

As you can see by the definition above, one reason for this is that most search engines use indexes developed by machines. Therefore they are indexing terms not concepts. The search engine cannot tell the difference between the keyword "crack" to mean a split in the sidewalk and "crack" referring to crack cocaine. To use search engines properly takes some skill, and this chapter will provide tips to help you use search engines more effectively. First, however, let's look at the different types of search engines with examples:

TYPES OF SEARCH ENGINES

TYPE	DESCRIPTION	EXAMPLES
1st Generation	• Non-evaluative, do not evaluate results in terms of content or authority. • Return results ranked by relevancy alone (number of times the term(s) entered appear, usually on the first paragraph or page of the site)	AltaVista (www.altavista.com) Excite (www.excite.com) HotBot (www.HotBot.com) Ixquick Metasearch (ixquick.com) Lycos (www.lycos.com)
2nd Generation	• More creative in displaying results. • Results are ordered by characteristics such as: concept, document type, Web site, popularity, etc. rather than relevancy.	Ask (www.ask.com) Direct Hit (www.directhit.com) Google! (www.google.com) HotLinks (www.hotlinks.com) Simplifind (www.simpli.com) SurfWax (www.surfwax.com) Also see Meta-Search engines below. EVALUATIVE SEARCH ENGINES About.Com (www.about.com) WebCrawler (www.webcrawler.com)
Commercial Portals	• Provide additional features such as: customized news, stock quotations, weather reports, shopping, etc. • They want to be used as a "one stop" Web guide. • They profit from prominent advertisements and fees charged to featured sites.	GONetwork (www.go.com) Google Web Directory (directory.google.com) LookSmart (www.looksmart.com) My Starting Point (www.stpt.com) Open Directory Project (dmoz.org) NetNow (www.inetnow.com) Yahoo! (www.yahoo.com)
Meta-Search Engines	Run searches on multiple search engines.	There are different types of meta-search engines. See the next 2 boxes.

(continued)

TYPES OF SEARCH ENGINES, *continued*

TYPE	DESCRIPTION	EXAMPLES
Meta-Search Engines *Integrated Result*	• Display results for search engines in one list. • Duplicates are removed. • Only portions of results from each engine are returned.	Beaucoup.com (www.beaucoup.com) Highway 61 (www.highway61.com) Cyber411 (www.cyber411. com) Mamma (www.mamma.com) MetaCrawler (www. metacrawler.com) Visisimo (www.vivisimo.com) Northern Light (www.nlsearch.com) SurfWax (www.surfwax.com)
Meta-Search Engines *Non-Integrated Results*	• Comprehensive search. • Displays results from each search engine in separate results sets. • Duplicates remain. • You must sift through all the sites.	Dogpile (www.dogpile.com) GoHip (www.gohip.com) Searchalot (www.searchalot.com) ProFusion (www. profusion.com)

QUICK TIPS FOR MORE EFFECTIVE USE OF SEARCH ENGINES

1. Use a search engine:
   - When you have a narrow idea to search.
   - When you want to search the full text of countless Web pages
   - When you want to retrieve a large number of sites
   - When the features of the search engine (like searching particular parts of the Web) help with your search

2. Always use Boolean Operators to combine terms. Searching on a single term is a sure way to retrieve a very large number of Web pages, few, if any, of which are on target.
   - Always check search engine's HELP feature to see what symbols are used for the operators as these vary (e.g., some engines use the & or + symbol for AND).
   - Boolean Operators include:
     AND to narrow search and to make sure that **both** terms are included
       e.g., children AND violence
     OR to broaden search and to make sure that **either** term is included
       e.g., child OR children OR juveniles
     NOT to **exclude** one term
       e.g., eclipse NOT lunar

3. Use appropriate symbols to indicate important terms and to indicate phrases (Best Bet for Constructing a Search According to Cohen (1999): Use a plus sign (+) in front of terms you want to retrieve: +solar +eclipse. Place a phrase in double quotation marks: "solar eclipse" Put together: "+solar eclipse" "+South America").

4. Use word stemming (a.k.a. truncation) to find all variations of a word (check search engine HELP for symbols).
   • If you want to retrieve child, child's, or children use child* (some engines use other symbols such as !, #, or $)
   • Some engines automatically search singular and plural terms, check HELP to see if yours does.

5. Since search engines only search a portion of the Web, use several search engines or a meta-search engine to extend your reach.

6. Remember search engines are generally mindless drones that do not evaluate. Do not rely on them to find the best Web sites on your topic, use *subject directories* or meta-sites to enhance value (see below).

Finding Those Diamonds in the Desert: Using Subject Directories and Meta-sites

Although some search engines, like WebCrawler (www.webcrawler.com) do evaluate the Web sites they index, most search engines do not make any judgment on the worth of the content. They just return a long—sometimes very long—list of sites that contained your keyword. However, *subject directories* exist that are developed by human indexers, usually librarians or subject experts, and are defined by Cohen (1999) as follows:

> "A subject directory is a service that offers a collection of links to Internet resources submitted by site creators or evaluators and organized into subject categories. Directory services use selection criteria for choosing links to include, though the selectivity varies among services (p. 27)."

World Wide Web Subject directories are useful when you want to see sites on your topic that have been reviewed, evaluated, and selected for their authority, accuracy, and value. They can be real time savers for students, since subject directories weed out the commercial, lightweight, or biased Web sites.

Metasites are similar to subject directories, but are more specific in nature, usually dealing with one scholarly field or discipline. Some examples of subject directories and meta-sites are found in the table on the next page.

SMART SEARCHING—SUBJECT DIRECTORIES AND META-SITES

TYPES—SUBJECT DIRECTORIES	EXAMPLES
General, covers many topics	Access to Internet and Subject Resources (www2.lib.udel.edu/subj/) Best Information on the Net (BIOTN) (http://library.sau.edu/bestinfo/) INFOMINE: Scholarly Internet Resource Collections (http://infomine.ucr.edu/) Librarian's Index to the Internet (www.lii.org/) Martindale's "The Reference Desk" (www.martindalecenter.com) PINAKES: A Subject Launchpad (www.hw.ac.uk/libWWW/irn/pinakes/pinakes.html) Refdesk.com (www.refdesk.com) Search Engines and Subject Directories (College of New Jersey) (www.tcnj.edu/~library/research/internet_search.html) Scout Report Archives (www.scout.cs.wisc.edu/archives) WWW Virtual Library (http://vlib.org)
Subject Oriented	
• Communication Studies	The Media and Communication Studies Site (www.aber.ac.uk/media) University of Iowa Department of Communication Studies (www.uiowa.edu/~commstud/resources)
• Cultural Studies	Sara Zupko's Cultural Studies Center (www.popcultures.com)
• Education	Educational Virtual Library (www.csu.edu.au/education/library.html) ERIC [Education ResourcesInformation Center] (www.eduref.org) Kathy Schrock's Guide for Educators (http://kathyschrock.net/abceval/index.htm)
• Journalism	Journalism Resources (https://bailiwick.lib.uiowa.edu/journalism/) Journalism and Media Criticism page (www.chss.montclair.edu/english/furr/media.html)
• Literature	Norton Web Source to American Literature (www.wwnorton.com/naal) Project Gutenberg [Over 3,000 full text titles] (www.gutenberg.org)

SMART SEARCHING, *continued*

TYPES—SUBJECT DIRECTORIES	EXAMPLES
• Medicine & Health	PubMed [National Library of Medicine's index to Medical journals, 1966 to present] (www.ncbi.nlm.nih.gov/PubMed/) RxList: The Internet Drug Index (http://rxlist.com) Go Ask Alice (www.goaskalice.columbia.edu) [Health and sexuality]
• Technology	CNET.com (www.cnet.com)

Choose subject directories to ensure that you are searching the highest quality Web pages. As an added bonus, subject directories periodically check Web links to make sure that there are fewer dead ends and out-dated links.

Another closely related group of sites are the *Virtual Library sites,* also referred to as Digital Library sites (see the table below). Hopefully, your campus library has an outstanding Web site for both on-campus and off-campus access to resources. If not, there are

VIRTUAL LIBRARY SITES

PUBLIC LIBRARIES

• Internet Public Library	www.ipl.org
• Library of Congress	http://lcweb.loc.gov/homepage/lchp.html
• New York Public Library	www.nypl.org

University/College Libraries

• Case Western	www.cwru.edu/uclibraries.html
• Dartmouth	www.dartmouth.edu/~library
• Duke	www.lib.duke.edu/
• Franklin & Marshall	www.library.fandm.edu
• Harvard	www.harvard.edu/museums/
• Penn State	www.libraries.psu.edu
• Stanford	www.slac.stanford.edu/FIND/spires.html
• ULCA	www.library.ucla.edu

Other

• Perseus Project [subject specific— classics, supported by grants from corporations and educational institutions]	www.perseus.tufts.edu

several virtual library sites that you can use, although you should realize that some of the resources would be subscription based, and not accessible unless you are a student of that particular university or college. These are useful because, like the subject directories and meta-sites, experts have organized Web sites by topic and selected only those of highest quality.

You now know how to search for information and use search engines more effectively. In the next section, you will learn more tips for evaluating the information that you found.

BIBLIOGRAPHY FOR FURTHER READING

Books

Basch, Reva. (1996). *Secrets of the Super Net Searchers.*

Berkman, Robert I. (2000). *Find It Fast: How to Uncover Expert Information on Any Subject Online or in Print.* NY: HarperResource.

Glossbrenner, Alfred & Glossbrenner, Emily. (1999). *Search Engines for the World Wide Web,* 2nd Ed. Berkeley, CA: Peachpit Press.

Hock, Randolph, & Berinstein, Paula. (1999). *The Extreme Searcher's Guide to Web Search Engines: A Handbook for the Serious Searcher.* Information Today, Inc.

Miller, Michael. (2000). *Complete Idiot's Guide to Yahoo!* Indianapolis, IN: Que.

Miller, Michael. (2000). *Complete Idiot's Guide to Online Search Secrets.* Indianapolis, IN: Que.

Paul, Nora, Williams, Margot, & Hane, Paula. (1999). *Great Scouts!: Cyber-Guides for Subject Searching on the Web.* Information Today, Inc.

Radford, Marie, Barnes, Susan, & Barr, Linda. (2001). *Web Research: Selecting, Evaluating, and Citing* Boston. Allyn and Bacon.

Journal Articles

Cohen, Laura B. (1999, August). The Web as a research tool: Teaching strategies for instructors. *CHOICE Supplement 3,* 20–44.

Cohen, Laura B. (August 2000). Searching the Web: The Human Element Emerges. *CHOICE Supplement 37,* 17–31.

Introna, Lucas D., & Nissenbaum, Helen. (2000). Shaping the web: Why the politics of search engines matters. The Information Society, Vol. 16, No. 3, pp. 169–185.

Evaluating Sources on the Web

Congratulations! You've found a great Web site. Now what? The Web site you found seems like the perfect Web site for your research.

But, are you sure? Why is it perfect? What criteria are you using to determine whether this Web site suits your purpose?

Think about it. Where else on earth can anyone "publish" information regardless of the *accuracy, currency,* or *reliability* of the information? The Internet has opened up a world of opportunity for posting and distributing information and ideas to virtually everyone, even those who might post misinformation for fun, or those with ulterior motives for promoting their point of view. Armed with the information provided in this guide, you can dig through the vast amount of useless information and misinformation on the World Wide Web to uncover the valuable information. Because practically anyone can post and distribute their ideas on the Web, you need to develop a new set of *critical thinking skills* that focus on the evaluation of the quality of information, rather than be influenced and manipulated by slick graphics and flashy moving java script.

Before the existence of online sources, the validity and accuracy of a source was more easily determined. For example, in order for a book to get to the publishing stage, it must go through many critiques, validation of facts, reviews, editorial changes and the like. Ownership of the information in the book is clear because the author's name is attached to it. The publisher's reputation is on the line too. If the book turns out to have incorrect information, reputations and money can be lost. In addition, books available in a university library are further reviewed by professional librarians and selected for library purchase because of their accuracy and value to students. Journal articles downloaded or printed from online subscription services, such as Infotrac, ProQuest, EbscoHost, or other fulltext databases, are put through the same scrutiny as the paper versions of the journals.

On the World Wide Web, however, Internet service providers (ISPs) simply give Web site authors a place to store information. The Web site author can post information that may not be validated or tested for accuracy. One mistake students typically make is to assume that all information on the Web is of equal value. Also, in the rush to get assignments in on time, students may not take the extra time to make sure that the information they are citing is accurate. It is easy just to cut and paste without really thinking about the content in a critical way. However, to make sure you are gathering accurate information and to get the best grade on your assignments, it is vital that you develop your critical ability to sift through the dirt to find the diamonds.

Web Evaluation Criteria

So, here you are, at this potentially great site. Let's go though some ways you can determine if this site is one you can cite with confidence in your research. Keep in mind, ease of use of a Web site is an

Evaluating Web Sites Using
Five Criteria to Judge Web Site Content

Accuracy—How reliable is the information?

Authority—Who is the author and what are his or her credentials?

Objectivity—Does the Web site present a balanced or biased point of view?

Coverage—Is the information comprehensive enough for your needs?

Currency—Is the Web site up to date?

Use additional criteria to judge Web site content, including

- **Publisher, documentation, relevance, scope, audience, appropriateness of format,** and **navigation**
- Judging whether the site is made up of **primary (original) or secondary (interpretive) sources**
- Determining whether the information is **relevant** to your research

issue, but more important is learning how to determine the validity of data, facts, and statements for your use. The five traditional ways to verify a paper source can also be applied to your Web source: *accuracy, authority, objectivity, coverage,* and *currency.*

Content Evaluation

Accuracy.   Internet searches are not the same as searches of library databases because much of the information on the Web has not been edited, whereas information in databases has. It is your responsibility to make sure that the information you use in a school project is accurate. When you examine the content on a Web site or Web page, you can ask yourself a number of questions to determine whether the information is accurate.

1. Is the information reliable?
2. Do the facts from your other research contradict the facts you find on this Web page?
3. Do any misspellings and/or grammar mistakes indicate a hastily put together Web site that has not been checked for accuracy?
4. Is the content on the page verifiable through some other source? Can you find similar facts elsewhere (journals, books, or other online sources) to support the facts you see on this Web page?
5. Do you find links to other Web sites on a similar topic? If so, check those links to ascertain whether they back up the information you see on the Web page you are interested in using.
6. Is a bibliography of additional sources for research provided? Lack of a bibliography doesn't mean the page isn't accurate, but

having one allows you further investigation points to check the information.

7. Does the site of a research document or study explain how the data was collected and the type of research method used to interpret the data?

If you've found a site with information that seems too good to be true, it may be. You need to verify information that you read on the Web by crosschecking against other sources.

Authority. An important question to ask when you are evaluating a Web site is, "Who is the author of the information?" Do you know whether the author is a recognized authority in his or her field? Biographical information, references to publications, degrees, qualifications, and organizational affiliations can help to indicate an author's authority. For example, if you are researching the topic of laser surgery citing a medical doctor would be better than citing a college student who has had laser surgery.

The organization sponsoring the site can also provide clues about whether the information is fact or opinion. Examine how the information was gathered and the research method used to prepare the study or report. Other questions to ask include:

1. Who is responsible for the content of the page? Although a webmaster's name is often listed, this person is not necessarily responsible for the content.
2. Is the author recognized in the subject area? Does this person cite any other publications he or she has authored?
3. Does the author list his or her background or credentials (e.g., Ph.D. degree, title such as professor, or other honorary or social distinction)?
4. Is there a way to contact the author? Does the author provide a phone number or email address?
5. If the page is mounted by an organization, is it a known, reputable one?
6. How long has the organization been in existence?
7. Does the URL for the Web page end in the extension .edu or .org? Such extensions indicate authority compared to dotcoms (.com), which are commercial enterprises. (For example, www.cancer.com takes you to an online drugstore that has a cancer information page; www.cancer.org is the American Cancer Society Web site.)

A good idea is to ask yourself whether the author or organization presenting the information on the Web is an authority on the subject. If the answer is no, this may not be a good source of information.

Objectivity. Every author has a point of view, and some views are more controversial than others. Journalists try to be objective by providing both sides of a story. Academics attempt to persuade readers by presenting a logical argument, which cites other scholars' work. You need to look for two sided arguments in news and information sites. For academic papers, you need to determine how the paper fits within its discipline and whether the author is using controversial methods for reporting a conclusion.

Authoritative authors situate their work within a larger discipline. This background helps readers evaluate the author's knowledge on a particular subject. You should ascertain whether the author's approach is controversial and whether he or she acknowledges this. More important, is the information being presented as fact or opinion? Authors who argue for their position provide readers with other sources that support their arguments. If no sources are cited, the material may be an opinion piece rather than an objective presentation of information. The following questions can help you determine objectivity:

1. Is the purpose of the site clearly stated, either by the author or the organization authoring the site?
2. Does the site give a balanced viewpoint or present only one side?
3. Is the information directed toward a specific group of viewers?
4. Does the site contain advertising?
5. Does the copyright belong to a person or an organization?
6. Do you see anything to indicate who is funding the site?

Everyone has a point of view. This is important to remember when you are using Web resources. A question to keep asking yourself is, What is the bias or point of *view* being expressed here?

Coverage. Coverage deals with the breadth and depth of information presented on a Web site. Stated another way, it is about how much information is presented and how detailed the information is. Looking at the site map or index can give you an idea about how much information is contained on a site. This isn't necessarily bad. Coverage is a criteria that is tied closely to *your* research requirement. For one assignment, a given Web site may be too general for your needs. For another assignment, that same site might be perfect. Some sites contain very little actual information because pages are filled with links to other sites. Coverage also relates to objectivity. You should ask the following questions about coverage:

1. Does the author present both sides of the story or is a piece of the story missing?

2. Is the information comprehensive enough for your needs?
3. Does the site cover too much, too generally?
4. Do you need more specific information than the site can provide?
5. Does the site have an objective approach?

In addition to examining what is covered on a Web site, equally revealing is what is not covered. Missing information can reveal a bias in the material. Keep in mind that you are evaluating the information on a Web site for your research requirements.

Currency.   Currency questions deal with the timeliness of information. However, currency is more important for some topics than for others. For example, currency is essential when you are looking for technology related topics and current events. In contrast, currency may not be relevant when you are doing research on Plato or Ancient Greece. In terms of Web sites, currency also pertains to whether the site is being kept up to date and links are being maintained. Sites on the Web are sometimes abandoned by their owners. When people move or change jobs, they may neglect to remove theft site from the company or university server. To test currency ask the following questions:

1. Does the site indicate when the content was created?
2. Does the site contain a last revised date? How old is the date? (In the early part of 2001, a university updated their Web site with a "last updated" date of 1901! This obviously was a Y2K problem, but it does point out the need to be observant of such things!)
3. Does the author state how often he or she revises the information? Some sites are on a monthly update cycle (e.g., a government statistics page).
4. Can you tell specifically what content was revised?
5. Is the information still useful for your topic? Even if the last update is old, the site might still be worthy of use *if* the content is still valid for your research.

Relevancy to Your Research: Primary versus Secondary Sources

Some research assignments require the use of primary (original) sources. Materials such as raw data, diaries, letters, manuscripts, and original accounts of events can be considered primary material. In most cases, these historical documents are no longer copyrighted. The Web is a great source for this type of resource.

Information that has been analyzed and previously interpreted is considered a secondary source. Sometimes secondary sources are more appropriate than primary sources. If, for example, you are asked to analyze a topic or to find an analysis of a topic, a secondary source of an analysis would be most appropriate. Ask yourself the following questions to determine whether the Web site is relevant to your research:

1. Is it a primary or secondary source?
2. Do you need a primary source?
3. Does the assignment require you to cite different types of sources? For example, are you supposed to use at least one book, one journal article, and one Web page?

You need to think critically, both visually and verbally, when evaluating Web sites. Because Web sites are designed as multimedia hypertexts, nonlinear texts, visual elements, and navigational tools are added to the evaluation process.

Help in Evaluating Web Sites. One shortcut to finding high-quality Web sites is using subject directories and meta-sites, which select the Web sites they index by similar evaluation criteria to those just described. If you want to learn more about evaluating Web sites, many colleges and universities provide sites that help you evaluate Web resources. The following list contains some excellent examples of these evaluation sites:

- Evaluating Quality on the Net—Hope Tillman, Babson College www.hopetillman.com/findqual.html
- Critical Web Evaluation—Kurt W. Wagner, William Paterson University of New Jersey http://euphrates.wpunj.edu/faculty/wagnerk/
- Evalation Criteria—Susan Beck, New Mexico State University http://lib.nmsu.edu/instruction/evalcrit.html
- A Student's Guide to Research with the WWW www.slu.edu/departments/english/research/

Critical Evaluation Web Sites

WEB SITE AND URL	SOURCE
Critical Thinking in an Online World **www.library.ucsb.edu/untangle/ jones.html**	*Paper from "Untangling the Web"* 1996
Educom Review: Information **www.educause.edu/pub/er/review/ reviewArticles/31231.html**	*EDUCAUSE Literacy as a Liberal Art (1996 article)*

WEB SITE AND URL	SOURCE
Evaluating Web Sites **www.lib.purdue.edu/InternetEval**	*Purdue University Library*
Searching the Web **www.lehigh.edu/helpdesk/ useweb.html**	*Lehigh University*
Kathy Schrock's ABC's of Web Site Evaluation **www.kathyschrock.net/abceval/**	*Author's Web site*
Testing the Surf: Criteria for Evaluating Internet Information Sources **http://info.lib.uh.edu/pr/v8/n3/ smit8n3.html**	*University of Houston Libraries*
UCLA College Library Instruction: Thinking Critically about World Wide Web Resources **www.library.ucla.edu/libraries/ college/help/critical/**	*UCLA Library*
UG OOL: Judging Quality on the Internet **www.open.uoguelph.ca/resources/ skills/judging.html**	*University of Guelph*
Web Evaluation Criteria **http://lib.nmsu.edu/instruction/ evalcrit.html**	*New Mexico State University Library*
Web Page Credibility Checklist **www.park.pvt.k12.md.us/academics/ research/credcheck.htm**	*Park School of Baltimore*
Evaluating Web Sites for Educational Uses: Bibliography and Checklist **www.unc.edu/cit/guides/irg-49.html**	*University of North Carolina*
Evaluating Web Sites **www.lesley.edu/library/guides/ research/evaluating_web.html**	*Lesley University*

Tip: Can't seem to get a URL to work? If the URL doesn't begin with www, you may need to put the http:// in front of the URL. Usually, browsers can handle URLs that begin with www without the need to type in the "http://" but if you find you're having trouble, add the http://.

Documentation Guidelines for Online Sources

Your Citation for Exemplary Research

There's another detail left for us to handle—the formal citing of electronic sources in academic papers. The very factor that makes research on the Internet exciting is the same factor that makes referencing these sources challenging: their dynamic nature. A journal article exists, either in print or on microfilm, virtually forever. A document on the Internet can come, go, and change without warning. Because the purpose of citing sources is to allow another scholar to retrace your argument, a good citation allows a reader to obtain information from your primary sources, to the extent possible. This means you need to include not only information on when a source was posted on the Internet (if available) but also when you obtained the information.

The two arbiters of form for academic and scholarly writing are the Modern Language Association (MLA) and the American Psychological Association (APA); both organizations have established styles for citing electronic publications.

MLA Style

In the fifth edition of the *MLA Handbook for Writers of Research Papers,* the MLA recommends the following formats:

- **URLs:** URLs are enclosed in angle brackets (<>) and contain the access mode identifier, the formal name for such indicators as "http" or "ftp." If a URL must be split across two lines, break it only after a slash (/). Never introduce a hyphen at the end of the first line. The URL should include all the parts necessary to identify uniquely the file/document being cited.

  `<http://www.csun.edu/~rtvfdept/home/index.html>`

- **An online scholarly project or reference database:** A complete "online reference contains the title of the project or database (underlined); the name of the editor of the project or database (if given); electronic publication information, including version number (if relevant and if not part of the title), date of electronic publication or latest update, and name of any sponsoring institution or organization; date of access; and electronic address.

  `The Perseus Project`. Ed. Gregory R. Crane.
  `    Mar. 1997. Department of Classics,`
  `    Tufts University. 15 June 1998 <http://`
  `    www.perseus.tufts.edu/>.`

If you cannot find some of the information, then include the information that is available. The MLA also recommends that you print or download electronic documents, freezing them in time for future reference.

- **A document within a scholarly project or reference database:** It is much more common to use only a portion of a scholarly project or database. To cite an essay, poem, or other short work, begin this citation with the name of the author and the title of the work (in quotation marks). Then, include all the information used when citing a complete online scholarly project or reference database, however, make sure you use the URL of the specific work and not the address of the general site.

Cuthberg, Lori. "Moonwalk: Earthlings' Finest
    Hour." <u>Discovery Channel Online</u>. 1999.
    Discovery Channel. 25 Nov. 1999 <http://
    www.discovery.com/indep/newsfeatures/
    moonwalk/challenge.html>.

- **A professional or personal site:** Include the name of the person creating the site (reversed), followed by a period, the title of the site (underlined), or, if there is no title, a description such as Home page (such a description is neither placed in quotes nor underlined). Then, specify the name of any school, organization, or other institution affiliated with the site and follow it with your date of access and the URL of the page.

Packer, Andy. Home page. 1Apr. 1998 <http://
    www.suu.edu/~students/Packer.htm>.

Some electronic references are truly unique to the online domain. These include email, newsgroup postings, MUDs (multiuser domains) or MOOs (multiuser domains, object-oriented), and IRCs (Internet Relay Chats).

Email.   In citing email messages, begin with the writer's name (reversed) followed by a period, then the title of the message (if any) in quotations as it appears in the subject line. Next comes a description of the message, typically "Email to," and the recipient (e.g., "the author"), and finally the date of the message.

Davis, Jeffrey. "Web Writing Resources." Email
    to Nora Davis. 3 Jan. 2000.

Sommers, Laurice. "Re: College Admissions Prac-
    tices." Email to the author. 12 Aug. 1998.

List Servers and Newsgroups.   In citing these references, begin with the author's name (reversed) followed by a period. Next include the title of the document (in quotes) from the subject line, followed by the words "Online posting" (not in quotes). Follow this with the date of posting. For list servers, include the date of access, the name of the list (if known), and the online address of the list's moderator or administrator. For newsgroups, follow "Online posting" with the date of posting, the date of access, and the name of the newsgroup, prefixed with "news:" and enclosed in angle brackets.

```
Applebaum, Dale. "Educational Variables." Online
    posting. 29 Jan. 1998. Higher Education Dis-
    cussion Group. 30 Jan. 1993 <jlucidoj@unc.edu>.

Gostl, Jack. "Re: Mr. Levitan." Online posting.
    13 June 1997. 20 June 1997 <news:alt.edu.
    bronxscience>.
```

MUDs, MOOs, and IRCs.   Begin with the name of the speaker(s) followed by a period. Follow with the description and date of the event, the forum in which the communication took place, the date of access, and the online address. If you accessed the MOO or MUD through telnet, your citation might appear as follows:

```
Guest. Personal interview. 13 Aug. 1998.
    <telnet://du.edu:8888>.
```

For more information on MLA documentation style for online sources, check out their Web site at http://www.mla.org/style/sources.htm.

APA Style

The newly revised *Publication Manual of the American Psychological Association* (5th ed.) now includes guidelines for Internet resources. The manual recommends that, at a minimum, a reference of an Internet source should provide a document title or description, a date (either the date of publication or update or the date of retrieval), and an address (in Internet terms, a uniform resource locator, or URL). Whenever possible, identify the authors of a document as well. It's important to remember that, unlike the MLA, the APA does not include temporary or transient sources (e.g., letters, phone calls, etc.) in its "References" page, preferring to handle them in the text. The general suggested format is as follows:

Online periodical:

Author, A. A., Author, B. B., & Author,
C. C. (2000). Title of article. *Title of
Periodical, xx,* xxxxx. Retrieved month, day,
year, from source.

Online document:

Author, A. A. (2000). *Title of work.* Retrieved
month, day, year, from source.

Some more specific examples are as follows:

FTP (File Transfer Protocol) Sites. To cite files available for downloading via FTP, give the author's name (if known), the publication date (if available and if different from the date accessed), the full title of the paper (capitalizing only the first word and proper nouns), the date of access, and the address of the FTP site along with the full path necessary to access the file.

Deutsch, P. (1991) Archie: An electronic
directory service for the Internet. Retrieved
January 25, 2000 from File Transfer Protocol:
ftp://ftp.sura.net/pub/archie/docs/
whatis.archie

WWW Sites (World Wide Web). To cite files available for viewing or downloading via the World Wide Web, give the author's name (if known), the year of publication (if known and if different from the date accessed), the full title of the article, and the title of the complete work (if applicable) in italics. Include any additional information (such as versions, editions, or revisions) in parentheses immediately following the title. Include the date of retrieval and full URL (the http address).

Burka, L. P. (1993). A hypertext history of
multi-user dungeons. *MUDdex.* Retrieved
January 13, 1997 from the World Wide Web:
http://www.utopia.com/talent/lpb/muddex/essay/

Tilton, J. (1995). Composing good HTML (Vers.
2.0.6). Retrieved December 1, 1996 from the
World Wide Web: http://www.cs.cmu.edu/
~tilt/cgh/

Synchronous Communications (MOOs, MUDs, IRC, etc.).   Give the name of the speaker(s), the complete date of the conversation being referenced in parentheses, and the title of the session (if applicable). Next, list the title of the site in italics, the protocol and address (if applicable), and any directions necessary to access the work. Last, list the date of access, followed by the retrieval information. Personal interviews do not need to be listed in the References, but do need to be included in parenthetic references in the text (see the APA *Publication Manual*).

```
Cross, J. (1996, February 27). Netoric's Tuesday
    "cafe: Why use MUDs in the writing classroom?
    MediaMoo. Retrieved March 1, 1996 from File
    Transfer Protocol: ftp://daedalus.com/pub/
    ACW/NETORIC/catalog
```

Gopher Sites.   List the author's name (if applicable), the year of publication, the title of the file or paper, and the title of the complete work (if applicable). Include any print publication information (if available) followed by the protocol (i.e., gopher://). List the date that the file was accessed and the path necessary to access the file.

```
Massachusetts Higher Education Coordinating
    Council. (1994). Using coordination and
    collaboration to address change. Retrieved
    July 16, 1999 from the World Wide Web:
    gopher://gopher.mass.edu:170/
    00gopher_root%3A%5B_hecc%5D_plan
```

Email, Listservs, and Newsgroups.   Do not include personal email in the list of References. Although unretrievable communication such as email is not included in APA References, somewhat more public or accessible Internet postings from newsgroups or listservs may be included. See the APA *Publication Manual* for information on in-text citations.

```
Heilke, J. (1996, May 3). Webfolios. Alliance
    for Computers and Writing Discussion List.
    Retrieved December 31, 1996 from the World
    Wide Web: http://www.ttu.edu/lists/acw-1/
    9605/0040.html
```

Other authors and educators have proposed similar extensions to the APA style. You can find links to these pages at:

`www.psychwww.com/resource/apacrib.htm`

Remember, "frequently-referenced" does not equate to "correct" "or even "desirable." Check with your professor to see if your course or school has a preference for an extended APA style.

Research Tips for the Helping Professions

This section of the *ResearchNavigator.com Guide* will help students across the helping professions to find journals and articles to help them develop, research, and write papers related to their course work and professional practice. Readers will learn how to frame literature search questions, how to target databases related to their topics of study, how to select effective keywords for narrowing their search results, and how to select the best articles from among those retrieved. Readers will also learn when and how to use the *New York Times Search by Subject Archive* and the *"Best of the Web" link library*, as well as the links found in Part 4 of the *ResearchNavigator.com Guide*. Finally, this section will suggest strategies for using *ResearchNavigator.com* together with library resources to gather evidence-based information related to completion of course assignments and in particular, papers for courses in any discipline.

Students in social work and related helping professions should be familiar with a wide variety of information resources to conduct research for their course work and for their future practice activities. Knowledge for practice comes from a variety of sources, including the individual professions, related helping professions, and a variety of academic disciplines, including psychology, sociology, anthropology, economics, political science and more. *ContentSelect* makes it possible for students and practitioners to search scholarly materials across all of these areas and more by enabling students to search multiple databases simultaneously.

The movement across helping professions to *evidence-based practice* represents an approach to professional decision-making, which is informed by the review of evidence gathered in systematic ways. In contrast with earlier practice strategies that were based largely on practice wisdom, customary approaches and expert opinion, evidence-based helping professionals make decisions based on reviews of information derived from rigorous, repeated scientific knowledge. Rather than seeking out information that supports an already-formed opinion, professionals who practice in an evidence-based way seek out all the information available on a given problem and then select the best evidence from among the gathered information.

Complicating efforts to practice in an evidence-based way, students and practitioners in the helping professions are faced with a deluge of information in the 21st century. In addition to the large amounts of existing information available through scholarly journals, periodicals, and the World Wide Web, new information is being added at a breathtaking pace. While this situation is preferable to not having enough information on which to base practice decisions, information overload can serve to hinder effective decision-making by making it difficult to find the best evidence available. For example, much of the information available on the World Wide Web has not been scrutinized in the same way as has the information presented in peer-reviewed journals or even in accepted doctoral dissertations. Some of the information available is incomplete and inaccurate and there are contradictions in the information presented. Students and practitioners alike must be armed with efficient strategies for retrieving, selecting, and processing these burgeoning amounts of information so they can find the best evidence for making decisions about any given practice topic or problem.

In order to approach professional practice in an evidence-based kind of way, students and practitioners need to develop skills in asking questions, deriving keywords from these questions, using these keywords in systematic searches of databases, choosing the best available evidence and avoiding the use of poor quality or incomplete evidence, and assessing the effectiveness of practice activities used. While a complete review of these critical skills is beyond the purview of this *ResearchNavigator.com Guide*, an examination of the first three of these steps will help students make best use of all the tools available to them in the *ResearchNavigator.com*.

Framing Literature Search Questions

The first step in retrieving information relevant to professional helping practice is the development of a well-formed question for guiding literature retrieval tasks. Without a well-formulated question, the search for information becomes a needlessly time-consuming and arduous task. Well-formed questions lead to the selection and utilization of keywords that can both assist in sifting through the huge amount of information available and find the most relevant articles and other material for a particular topic.

The range of topics related to professional practice is enormous, ranging from influences on behavior of individuals, to the management of organizations, to implementation of policy on a community, state, national or global scale. Regardless of the level of topic being studied, however, the formulation of questions to help guide the information retrieval process remains consistent. There are three basic types of questions that are asked of the body of evidence available to helping professionals: Description questions, which ask for descriptive information about a given problem and/or population; Relationship questions, which ask about how characteristics of individuals within a given population relate to other characteristics of these individuals or the environment in which they live; and Effectiveness questions, which ask about how well particular practice interventions or social policies work to solve specific problems for specific populations.

Description questions are those that can help students and practitioners discover the nature and extent of social problems. For example, we might want to understand the extent of adult illiteracy within a particular community and the impact of this problem on the lives of those experiencing it. The range of research available to answer these descriptive questions includes anecdotal case studies (individual examples of social problems are described), larger-scale qualitative studies (which typically provide more rigorous information on a somewhat larger scale than case studies), and surveys (which usually ask more limited questions of a much larger sample of the population). Generally, large surveys represent the best evidence for generalizing about groups of people and rigorous qualitative studies represent the best information available for an in-depth understanding of the impact of social problems on individuals.

Relationship questions ask about the correlations between variables associated with particular populations and social problems. For example, we may wish to understand if adult illiteracy is associated with poverty or if it appears to be associated with increased risk of addiction or criminal behavior and incarceration. While students and practitioners examining the literature pertinent to such questions might find some qualitative studies of people with adult illiteracy, the best evidence available for examining these questions will be relatively large sample quantitative surveys.

Finally, effectiveness questions ask about how well practice interventions and social policies accomplish the objectives for which they are intended. For example, students and practitioners might be interested in understanding interventions to address the problem of adult illiteracy. The literature will provide information about what these interventions look like and how to apply them and provide outcome data to demonstrate the effectiveness of these interventions. Both types of information are important because we want to know both which intervention approaches are the most efficacious and how to implement these interventions. The best evidence for effectiveness of interventions can be found in meta-analyses, which summarize the results across a number of high quality studies. Meta-analyses are considered stronger evidence than any single study because while any individual study is subject to various sources of confounding variables, findings from a number of such studies are less subject to such invalidity. In the absence of meta-analyses, which are a relatively new strategy for compiling evidence, randomized controlled experimental evaluation studies represent the best evidence available for intervention effectiveness.

For any of these types of questions, there is a basic formula for asking a question, which will lead you to the selection of helpful keywords. Each question will involve, at a minimum, specification of the client population in which you are interested, the problem in which you are interested, and the desired outcome. For example, in descriptive questions, you want to specify a population, such as adults, a problem, such as illiteracy, and an outcome, such as a description of the educational experiences of these adults. One such question might be: For adults with illiteracy, what will a survey reveal about their educational backgrounds?

For relationship questions, a well-formulated question would look very much the same as for a description question, but would specify additional elements. For example, we may be interested in learning about the relationship of ethnicity, educational attainment of parents, and the influence of learning disabilities on adult illiteracy. One resulting question may be: For adults, does the presence of a learning disability influence the development of adult illiteracy?

For effectiveness questions, well-formed questions also follow the same pattern as for the previous two types of questions, but ask which is the best intervention, policy, or program to produce a given outcome, how well a particular intervention, policy or program does in producing a particular outcome, or which of two (or more) interventions, policies, or programs are more effective in producing a particular outcome. Example questions might include: For adults with illiteracy, which is the best intervention to produce reading at a 4th grade level? For adults with illiteracy, how well does computer-assisted instruction work to bring learners to a 4th grade reading level? For adults with illiteracy, is classroom-based learning or computer-assisted instruction more effective at bringing learners to a 4th grade reading level?

To summarize, to develop a well-formed question for literature searches, students must specify a population, a problem, attributes or concepts to be described, variables to be examined, or interventions, policies or programs to be implemented, and the outcomes of interest. Once these questions are specified, students will be better able to target appropriate *ContentSelect* databases and select keywords to enable their systematic search of these databases.

Targeting ContentSelect Databases

Once a well-formed question has been specified, students can select which of the many *ContentSelect* databases to access for their literature search. The question of which databases to select depends largely on the population or problem being addressed within the question being asked. Because social workers and other helping professionals deal with a full spectrum of target/client systems, a wide variety of human problems, and also work collaboratively with a range of other helping professionals, literature pertaining to the well-formed questions developed in the previous step may be found in any number of databases.

Certainly, every *ContentSelect* search should include the Helping Professions Journals database. Journals included in this database include those from social work and related helping professions. Topics covered by these journals include those devoted to individual professions (e.g., *Journal of Social Work Practice, American Journal of Family Therapy,* and *Counseling Psychology Quarterly*), those relating to fields of practice (e.g., *American Journal of Criminal Justice, Disabilities Studies Quarterly, Journal of Mental Health Counseling,* and *Journal of Children & Poverty*), those covering populations with whom helping professionals work (e.g., *Affilia: Journal of Women & Social Work, Journal of Addictions & Offender Counseling, Journal of Muslim Minority Affairs,* and *Multicultural Perspectives*), those relating to practice methods (e.g., *Journal of Sex & Marital Therapy, International Journal of Psychotherapy,* and *International Forum of Psychoanalysis*), and those devoted to problems with which helping professionals work (e.g., *AIDS Reader, American Journal on Addictions, Eating Disorders,* and *Journal of Interpersonal Violence*). Even if the Helping Professions Journals database is the only one searched by students, it is sufficiently comprehensive and broad in scope to locate some literature related to the question asked.

Depending on the topics of interest, however, students will want to search additional databases pertinent to their questions. For example, students looking for theoretical perspectives on helping professional practice may wish to search for articles in disciplinary databases, such as the Anthropology Journals database. For learning about the implications of various cultures for professional helping practice, the Political Science Journals database would be useful. For examining social policy issues related to practice, the Psychology Journals database may provide more in-depth knowledge about the theoretical and research bases for individual, family, and group-based interventions, and the Sociology Journals database may help students locate more in-depth information about interventions with larger social units.

In addition to accessing the Helping Profession Journal and disciplinary databases, students may also wish to tap into other databases to make their searches more thorough. For example, students with interests in practice with individuals who have various disabilities may find the Communication Sciences Disorders Journals database to be useful. Many helping professionals work in educational settings, and students with topics in this area of practice will find the Education Journal database critical to finding information related to their research. Students who are interested in practice with juvenile delinquents or adult criminal offenders will find that the Criminal Justice Journal database is the best source of articles to inform their research. Finally, students interested in helping professional practice in health settings will find the Nursing and Health Professions Journal database to be a rich source of articles pertinent to their topics.

In summary, it is important for students to recognize that the use of multiple databases within *ContentSelect* is the most effective strategy for finding articles relevant to any given topic. While many of these databases overlap somewhat in terms of which journals they contain, using multiple databases will maximize the likelihood that students find the best information available. The correct databases to use will vary with topics of interest, and with experience, students will gain proficiency in determining which databases will bring back the most relevant results.

Selecting Keywords

Once the appropriate databases for your search have been selected, it is time to choose keywords that will help narrow the literature to articles pertaining to your topic of interest. In a simple search, as will be illustrated later, all information is accessed with one set of terms entered into the search field. In an advanced search, multiple searches can be combined to refine the literature search further.

The well-formed question that was developed as the first step in the search process should be utilized in the selection of keywords. In the case of a simple search, it is most appropriate to combine keywords related to the population, problem, or issue being addressed and perhaps the intervention, program, or policy being investigated. In the case of an advanced search, where several searches can be combined, students should select keywords that relate to the population, problem, intervention, or outcome under investigation, as appropriate to their well-formed question, but then can expand or limit their searches through combinations of previous searches.

It is important to consider synonyms for the keywords being used, because there is a good chance that authors and journals use different words to describe the same concepts. For example, students who are interested in learning about interventions for drug abuse will find that "drug abuse" will locate only some articles relevant to their topic. However, if they also use "substance abuse," "addiction," "chemical dependency," or the names of substances, such as "methamphetamine," "heroin," "cocaine," or "alcohol," they will uncover many other articles in their search. Some of these synonyms can be found using a thesaurus as a reference, but one of the best ways to find keyword synonyms is to begin reading and search for other synonyms as they are discovered within articles.

The power of keywords to find articles relevant to a given research topic can be enhanced by careful utilization of Boolean operators, truncation symbols, and wildcard symbols, as discussed earlier in this guide.

Sample Searches

To illustrate the process of asking questions, selecting databases, and choosing keywords that will streamline your search, we will now walk through three types of search strategies, a visual search, a basic search, and an advanced search. To illustrate these various search strategies, we will use the example of therapeutic treatment of depression. Specifically, what is the most promising therapy approach for treating depression?

As discussed, it is important to first develop a well-formed question to guide the search. As framed, it would appear that this is an *effectiveness* question. As discussed above, this means that we want to specify the population, problem, and desired outcome. Here is where the first of several important decisions need to be made. For whom is this intervention desired? Is it for everyone? Is it for adults, adolescents, men, women, African-Americans, people in poverty? For sake of the illustration, let's say that we are interested in finding the most effective intervention to alleviate depression for adolescent females. Therefore, the population is adolescent females who have depression, and we are looking for the most effective therapeutic intervention for alleviating that depression.

The next step in our search is to choose the best databases for locating literature pertinent to the search. As always, we will use the Helping Professions Journals database. In addition to that, we may also want to access the Psychology Journals database, because that database includes both clinical psychology journals and journals, which may contain articles that explain the theoretical basis for interventions addressing depression.

Finally, we want to select the best keywords to streamline our literature search. Returning to our original question, it would appear that we need to specify the population (adolescent females), the problem (depression), and the intervention (therapy). Further, we probably want to think about possible synonyms for the keywords we have selected. For example, some synonyms for "adolescent" might be "teenage" or "young adult." Synonyms for "females" might be "girls" or "women." "Depression" is a diagnostic term, and so we probably don't need to think about synonyms, but "therapy" may not find us all the articles that we want to access. Good synonyms for "therapy" might be "intervention" or "treatment." Armed with these keywords and synonyms, we can proceed with our three search strategies.

ContentSelect's Visual Search

The old adage, "a picture is worth a thousand words," illustrates the utility of *ContentSelect's* visual search capability. For those of use who are visual learners, this may be the easiest strategy for finding articles relevant to our topic. From your ResearchNavigator.com start page, open *ContentSelect*, and select the Helping Profession Journals and the Psychology Journals databases using your CTRL or Command key. Type "depression" into the keyword box. We will see in a moment why this is the only keyword we need to use for a visual search! Click the "Go" button.

You will see immediately that this search brings up many articles, but that many or most of them are not relevant to psychotherapeutic interventions for depression with adolescent females. Click the "Visual Search" tab, and reenter "depression" in the search field box.

This results in a circle containing several circles, each of which we will now explore. First, it is important to check the filters to make sure that we are accessing all the available literature. Use the toggle switch and move it to the left to access all of the articles available in the *ContentSelect* databases.

Next, let's look at the "Affective Disorders Depression" circle by clicking on it. That doesn't seem like exactly what we're looking for, so use the "Zoom Back" tab to return to the top level. The "Antidepressants Depression," "Children Depression," "Depressed Persons," "General," "Mental Geriatric Psychiatry," "Mental Medicine," and "Stress Psychology" circles all seem like they might be relevant somehow, but not exactly what we are looking for.

Let's open the "Mental Health" circle by clicking on it. This looks more promising! An article on the first level of this circle discusses a strengths perspective for working with an adolescent with depression. Save this article citation and zoom back out to see what else could be found.

Clicking on the "Depressed Persons" circle, we can see an article on gender differences in adolescent depression. While this is not exactly what we are looking for, it may contain references or additional information we need, and so it too should be saved. Moving in further by clicking on the "More" circle, we see an article comparing depressive symptoms in children and adolescents, which might also be saved as background information, and another article on MH (Mental Health) intervention for adolescents, which might be even more directly relevant, and so should be saved.

Without a lot of sweat, we have located several articles that might be useful for our topic. Each of these articles should be read carefully, and references checked for additional articles that relate to finding the best psychotherapeutic interventions for helping adolescent females who have depression. As we will discuss later, some of the references we find within these articles are in journals not found within *ContentSelect*. Do not despair! This is where your local or academic library will be essential to completing your search.

Conducting a Basic Search

To conduct a basic search, we need to go back to go back to our well-formed question and again select the one best keyword for our search, which is "depression." We also need to select the two databases most appropriate to this search, which are the Helping Professions Journals and the Psychology Journals databases. After clicking the "Go" button, *ContentSelect* defaults to the basic search page, and we see a listing of more than 3,500 documents related to depression.

It would take us much too long to go through all of these citations to find the best articles available. The basic search has two strategies that can help us narrow down the field to find relevant articles. One option would be to use the terms in the left hand, yellow column to narrow the results. For example, clicking on "MENTAL health" narrows the list to 250 documents, and then clicking on "DEPRESSED persons" further narrows the list to 124. While we might luck out using this strategy and eventually find what we are looking for, this strategy is really the same as using the circles within the visual search, and represents no advantage over that strategy.

The advantage of the basic search over the visual search is the ability to use Boolean operators, truncation and wildcard symbols, parentheses, quotation symbols and the like to narrow the search right in the search field. We can also search for synonyms for our search terms at the same time!

Returning to our well-formed question and synonyms terms, we can revise the search field as follows: Depression AND (adolescen* OR teenage) AND (treatment OR therapy) AND (female OR girl). This search string uses the AND operator to narrow our results to therapeutic treatment of depression for adolescent females. Further, the OR operator is used within parentheses to group together the terms for adolescent, therapy, and females with common synonyms. Finally, the asterisk symbol (*) is used as a truncation symbol to expand the term "adolescent," so that "adolescence" might also be found in the search. You can use these special operators to refine the search in many different ways. You can find these suggestions within the help screen for the basic search.

Clicking on the "search" button, we can see that using the above search terms results in 17 document citations. Scrolling through these citations, we find several articles that might be relevant to the topic, but only one, on the developmental origins and treatment needs of female adolescents with depression, is most closely related. Because this is a full-text article available through *ContentSelect*, we can click on the "PDF Full Text" icon and view the document directly!

Looking at the article, we can see a section of the introduction that deals with the recent status of research on treatment for this population, along with references to specific articles on this topic. While this article is important for our topic, the references listed may have more direct relevancy for our search, and should be worth looking into.

Conducting an Advanced Search

The main advantage of *ContentSelect*'s advanced search strategy over its basic search strategy is in the capability of using search history to guide the search incrementally. This means that instead of entering all of the keywords and synonyms into the search field as in the basic search, terms can be entered individually, and then the results of individual searches can be added using OR or AND. This permits the searcher to revise individual components of the search one at a time, allowing for greater flexibility and precision of search options.

Using the same well-formed question and starting from the *ContentSelect* start page, select the same two databases we used for the last two searches, the Helping Profession Journals and the Psychology Journals databases. Type "depression" into the search field, and click the "Go" button. This brings us back to the basic search page and the same initial results we saw in the previous search.

Now, click on the "Advanced Search" tab. This brings up the "Refine Search" page. Unclicking the box for "full text" will get you both citations you can follow up with from your local or academic library as well as full text articles. Click the box next to "Also search for related words," type "depression" in the search field, and click the "Search" box. This brings up the same results seen in the basic search. To observe how the search history works, click on the "Search History/Alerts" tab above the results. What you will see is a summary of the first search, which might later be revised to change search terms, limiters, expanders, and databases accessed.

Here is where the search strategy begins to diverge from that of the basic search. Clearing the search field with the "Clear" button, now type "adolescen* OR teenage*" and click the "Search" box, making sure that the "Also search for related words" is checked and the "full text" option is unchecked. This search should bring up even more citations than the previous search. Check the search history tab to observe that there are now two entries in the search history; one for each of the searches conducted.

The above process can then be repeated for each of the rest of the keywords derived from our well-formed question. After again clearing the search field box by clicking the "Clear" button, enter "treat* OR therap* OR interven*" to get a wide variety of treatment terms, and click the "Search" button. Next, clear the search field using the "Clear" button, enter "female* OR girl*" and then click "Search."

Clicking on the "Search History/Alerts" tab will show four different searches, each with varying numbers of citations. We are now going to combine these searches using the ADD operator so that we will locate only those articles that have all four sets of terms in their descriptors.

Start by clearing the search field again with the "Clear" button. Scroll down to the bottom of the page. Select each of the searches that we want to use in the combined search, in this case all four, by clicking in the leftmost column next to each search. At the top of the search history, make sure that "add" is selected in the drop down menu, and click the "Add" button. The term "S4 And S3 And S2 And S1" will now appear in the search field. Click the "Search" button. This will result in about 25 citations, several of which are full text and many of which are directly relevant to our search topic.

As indicated earlier, this ability to combine searches through the search history is what makes the advanced search option within *ContentSelect* so attractive. Should the combination of searches result in too many citations, it is possible to add another search, for example for "meta analysis" to see if that would further refine the results. Should the combination of searched result in too few citations, however, individual searches can be eliminated from the combined search, thus resulting in more citations. One of the searches that might be considered for elimination would be that for "adolescent," with the result that the search would turn up studies for adult females as well as those for adolescent females. Alternatively, one could eliminate the search for "female," with the result that articles relevant to treatment of depression for adolescents of both genders.

Selecting the Best Available Evidence

In general, searches using the three strategies discussed above will uncover a large number of articles. How can students decide which articles are best? There are at least two criteria by which to make this decision. First, students should carefully examine where these articles are published, and second, students should judge articles based on the quality and rigor of the study methods used to produce them.

In judging an article quality, students should weigh articles published in peer-reviewed journals more heavily than those published in other types of publications, such as magazines and newspapers. What is meant by "peer-reviewed" is that articles are reviewed, usually with author-identifying information hidden, by at least two scholars recognized as having some expertise in the topic about which the article is written. While the peer-review process is not fool-proof, it is probably the best strategy researchers have available to them for exercising quality control over what types of articles get published in journals.

Fortunately, *ContentSelect* abstracts the leading journals within each discipline, and so students can be assured that the articles they find using it are of relatively good quality. However, students will almost always need to supplement their *ContentSelect* search with additional information from their local or academic libraries, and then they must exercise caution in selecting which articles to trust. In order to learn about the review process for a given journal, students might wish to look at a Web page for the journal and read about the process by which articles are selected for publication. If there is not a blind peer-review process in place by which to judge whether an article is worthy of publication, students should be extra cautious in utilizing the information contained in that article.

The second set of criteria pertains to the quality and rigor of the methods applied in the study. Earlier in this section, we discussed the types of research methods that might be appropriate to the type of question being asked. While curriculum content on research methods within each of the helping professions is necessary to help students critically analyze the research methods used to produce a given set of findings, you might ask yourself whether the research design is appropriate to the type of question you want to answer. For example, you may uncover an excellent qualitative study that interviews a number of adolescent females about their experiences with depression. If this article is published in a peer-reviewed journal, it is probably a well-done qualitative study, but it's not going to help the reader decide which interventions are the most effective for working with this population. In order to answer effectiveness questions, students should be seeking studies that utilize experimental or otherwise controlled designs or meta-analytic studies, which represent summarizations of a number of controlled studies. Similarly, if a student is writing a paper on the differences between adolescent males with depression and adolescent females with depression, experimental evaluations of interventions, no matter how high-quality, are not going to be as useful as qualitative, in-depth interviews or large scale surveys of the populations of interest.

The *New York Times* Search by Subject Archive

The *New York Times Search by Subject Archive* allows students to access articles published in that newspaper within the past 12 months. Like other newspapers, articles published in the *New York Times* differ from those published in peer-reviewed scholarly journals and abstracted in *ContentSelect* and other abstracting services. Newspaper reporters write for a living. They write under critical deadlines, and as we have learned in the recent past, do not always have the time to check reference materials carefully. However, articles in the *New York Times* may represent the very latest scientific findings because there is no need for a peer-review process, which typically delays the publication of scholarly journal articles. Therefore, it is often useful to begin a literature search with the *New York Times Search by Subject Archive*, although the material found there should be viewed with caution.

Articles found in the *New York Times* will usually be somewhat less specific than students in the helping professions will require for writing papers; however, they may be helpful in other ways. For example, information about the extent or ramifications of a social problem the student is addressing may be more current in the *New York Times* than in the scholarly journals. Also, news of new research findings may be published as a brief report in the *New York Times* many years before more rigorous information is available in the peer-reviewed journals. Students may wish to search for the researchers' names within articles already appearing in the scholarly journals to find research that has led to the current findings. Thus, the *New York Times Search by Subject Archive* may be the first stop for students starting to research a topic for a paper. With the limitations on the information to be retrieved always in mind, let's walk through an example search using the same topic as we used above.

Opening the *New York Times Search by Subject Archive* main window, the first thing we will notice is that content is organized by subject area, as opposed to within databases. For our search for information about interventions for working with adolescent females with depression, we should select subject areas that seem appropriate to the topic. Although we could probably just use "All," "Mental Health Services," "Psychology," "Social Work," and "Women's Studies" might quickly target the information we are seeking. With those topics highlighted, we found 14 articles related to depression, at least some of which are relevant to the topic. Because articles can be accessed for a period of only one year, results will vary from day to day. Interestingly, using "All" resulted in many more articles, but many or most of these were not relevant to our topic.

To summarize, the *New York Times Search by Subject Archive*, while never sufficient for a complete student research project, can help a student get off to a good start by giving the student a general impression of the topic and by providing clues about who has been doing the most promising research in a given area. Thus, this tool is an excellent adjunct to a student's research!

Using the "Best of the Web" Link Library

The World Wide Web is a mixed bag. Hundreds of thousands of new Web pages are posted on the Internet every day, and this number is increasing over time. The Internet might be described as anarchy, in that there is little or no restriction about who can publish work. While much of the information on the World Wide Web can be useful, much of it is published by individuals who are academically untrained and unqualified, and much of the information presented is incomplete, inaccurate, and inadequate for the purposes of a student's research.

Research Navigator's Best of the Web Links and the links found in Part IV of this guide, however, can be helpful in finding high quality information on the World Wide Web. These resources list only editorially reviewed and credible Web sites for research. Just as with using the *New York Times Search by Subject Archive*, students should consider information found on the internet to be subject to verification from more recognized and quality-controlled sources, such as articles published in peer-reviewed journals.

The *Links Library* can be accessed from the main search page within *Research Navigator*. Using the same well-formed question about effective treatments for adolescent females with depression, we first need to select one subject area within which to look for links to useful Web sites. As there is not yet a *Links Library* for the helping professions, we will use the subject area that would see most appropriate for our search, "Psychology—General Psychology." With that subject area highlighted, click the "Go" button.

Another browser window will open with letters of the alphabet across the top of the page, click on "D" and then click on "Depression." This opens yet another window with a series of annotated links, all relating to our topic of depression. The last link on the page is entitled "Treatment for Depression," and it indicates that it was "[d]esigned by a Canadian psychiatrist in collaboration with Canada-Japan Mental Health Exchange," and that "this site is part of a free encyclopedia of mental health information." Click that link.

The first thing we learn is that this site was authored by Phillip W. Long, M.D., and that it was updated on February 9, 1998. While we may take some comfort in its development by a physician, the fact that this site has not been updated since 1998 should make us suspect that the information presented is not up-to-date. Regardless, we might think of the information presented on this site as being good historical information about the treatment of depression.

Looking at Part 4 of this *Research Navigator Guide*, we might examine the section pertaining to Mental Health, in Part 4 of this guide. There, we will find a link to the National Institute of Mental Health (**http://www.nimh.nih.gov**). Type that link into your browser's search field and press enter to go to NIMH's site. Under "Health Information," there is a link to "Depression." Click that link, and a wide variety of information related to depression becomes instantly available. There is information of the definition of depression, on signs and symptoms of depression, and on treatment issues, as well as links to resource materials, depression research, and related information. By searching for links related to children and adolescents with depression, we were able to find some of the latest research related to the treatment of depression with adolescents, although we did not immediately find information specific to working with female adolescents. We were also able to find literature citations in the section on current research, which could be followed up in a local or academic library using a resource such as *PubMed*. Because this information is published on a government Website, we can be reassured of its credibility.

To summarize, there is much good information on the World Wide Web, but there is also a lot of inaccurate, out of date, or otherwise inadequate information. By following the links provided in *ResearchNavigator.com's Links Library* or those found in Part 4 of this guide. Students may be able to find some excellent resources that may then be verified by information from peer-reviewed journals.

P A R T **4**

Online Resources

Internet Sites Useful in Counseling

Psychiatry

PROFESSIONAL ORGANIZATIONS

American Psychiatric Association

http://www.psych.org

American Psychiatric Nurses Association

http://www.apna.org

This online resource containing legislative action alerts, government links, APNA membership, and professional resources.

National Association of Psychiatric Health Systems

http://www.naphs.org

This behavior health care systems Web site containing membership information and resources.

American Association of Geriatric Psychiatry

http://www.aagpgpa.org

This resource contains an AAGP bookstore, bulletins, consumer information, links to other online information, a member meeting place, and legal notices.

Psychiatric Disabilities, Employment, and the Americans with Disabilities Act Background Paper

http://www.wwws.princeton.edu/cgi-bin/
byteserv.prl/~ota/disk1/1994/9427/942701.PDF

This document evaluates current efforts under the ADA in the area of psychiatric disabilities and employment. This study was conducted by the Office of Technology Assessment.

AACP's Virtual Community Psychiatrist

http://www.communitypsychiatry.org

A publication of the American Association of Community Psychiatrists, this site contains links with additional psychiatric resources for community mental health.

American Association of Medical Review Office

http://www.aamro.com

This site contains links with educational programs, certification information, resources, and seminars.

DSM-IV Diagnoses and Codes

http://www.dr-bob.org/tips/dsm4a.html

This is an alphabetical listing of diagnoses and codes. There is also a corresponding numerical listing.

Professional Connections

LISTSERVS

CataList

http://www.lsotft.com/lists/listref.html

A catalogue of 26,789 public listserv lists on the Internet. Search for mailing lists of interest, and get information about listserv host sites.

Listserve list by Subject

http://www.mste.uiuc.edu/listservs/
subjectsearch.html

Global School Psychology Network

http://www.dac.neu.edu/cp/consult/

An innovative Internet Community dedicated to peer support, problem-solving assistance, professional development, and research.

Prevention & Treatment

http://journals.apa.org/prevention

Edited by Martin E.-P. Seligman *Prevention & Treatment* is also free and comes with an email discussion list for subscribers to discuss the latest in psychological and psychiatric outcome/treatment research. Also included is some information on the Planetree model of patient-centered health care that is emerging as an alternative to traditional managed care.

Counseling Today

http://www.counseling.org/Publications/
CounselingToday.aspx

The Web version of *Counseling Today* has been revamped with a new look and more importantly is updated throughout the week with the latest news affecting professional counseling.

Human Rights in Action!

http://www.un.org/Pubs/CyberSchoolBus/humanrights

The purpose of this site is to examine human rights within the context of education. Specifically, the discussion will attempt to examine the teaching of and learning about human rights within schools and the classroom.

CESNET-L

A moderated listserv concerning counselor education and supervision, discussions about research, theory, and development of program applications pertinent to counselor education or supervision are encouraged. The listserv is concerned with the preparation and supervision of counselors in agencies, school settings, and private

practice. To subscribe: subscribe CESNET-L@LISTSERV.KENT.EDU
your email address.

COUNSGRADS

COUNSGRADS has been developed to help graduate students
from across the country communicate with one another. Students can
talk about classes, internships, papers, and ideas about the profession. To sign up, send an email to: counsgrads@lists.acs.ohio-state.
edu with the following in the body of the message: subscribe COUN-
SGRADS jane smith.

Listserv Directories

http://www.mailbase.ac.uk
http://psychcentral.com/mail.htm

U.S. Department of Education

http://www.ed.gov

This U.S. Department of Education site includes an education ki-
osk, community updates, an EdInfo/listserv, Ed initiatives, Ed press
releases, Ed publications published within the last ninety days, sat-
ellite town meetings, speeches, and testimonies, White House education press releases and statements, National Center for Education
statistics, and school-to-work, safe and drug-free schools, Office of
Vocational and Adult Education, and National Library of Education
information.

At Health, Inc.

http://www.athealth.com

This newsletter is distributed to over 7,300 mental health
professionals.

DISCUSSION GROUPS AND BULLETIN BOARDS

The Network Observer

The file contains a single article from *The Network Observer,* entitled "The Art of Getting Help," which offers some guidelines about
using Internet discussion groups to ask for assistance with research
projects and the like. For a much longer paper that describes how to
use the Net to build a professional community, send a message that
looks like this:

To: rre-request@weber.ucsd.edu
Subject: archive send network

Network Observer is distributed through the Red Rock Eater News Service. To subscribe to RRE, send a message to the RRE server, rre-request@ weber.ucsd.edu, whose subject line reads "subscribe first name last name;" for example "Subject: subscribe Jane Doe." For more information about the Red Rock Eater, send a message to that same address with a subject line of "help." For back issues, use a subject line of "archive send index."

Psychotherapy Usenet Group

news:sci.psychology.psychotherapy

School Counseling

http://www.schoolcounselor.com

The schoolcounselor.com Web site offers a newsletter, counseling link database, and more.

TREATMENT SOFTWARE

Therascribe

http://www.therapyshop.com/TheraScribe/

Therascribe can produce treatment plans which are outstanding and contain all elements of JCAHO. Windows-based design.

Clinical Supervision Models

http://www.nbcc.org/

This is the NBCC Web site for their supervision certification and model.

The Values Realization Institute

http://valuesrealization.org

This nonprofit organization posts the following mission statement: The Values Realization Institute creates, supports, and empowers a network of people committed to using the Values Realization principles and concepts to positively impact the quality of life in our world community.

PROFESSIONAL ORGANIZATIONS

The American Psychological Association

http://www.apa.org

The American Psychological Society

http://www.psychologicalscience.org

American Association for Marriage and Family Therapy

http://www.aamft.org/

American Counseling Association

http://www.counseling.org

California Association of Marriage and Family Therapists

http://www.camft.org/

American Association for Therapeutic Humor

http://www.aath.org/

Association for Multicultural Counseling and Development

http://www.bgsu.edu/colleges/edhd/programs/AMCD/

American Academy of Counseling Psychology

http://www.aacop.net/

Association for Death Education and Counseling

http://www.adec.org/

Association for Humanistic Psychology

http://www.ahpweb.org/

Association for Transpersonal Psychology

http://www.atpweb.org/

American Music Therapy Association

http://www.musictherapy.org

American Association of Pastoral Counselors

http://www.aapc.org/

National Coalition of Arts Therapy Associations

http://www.nccata.org/

Sufi Psychological Association

http://www.sufi-psychology.org

Researching Online

Dual Diagnosis Online Dictionary of Mental Health

http://www.human-nature.com/odmh/dual.html

Sciacca hosts this Web site for co-occurring mental illness and substance disorders. Complete articles and chapters may be read and downloaded. It also contains a search engine and mailing lists.

BOOKSTORES

Amazon.com

http://www.amazon.com

This excellent online book store offers some great savings!

Jason Aronson, Inc

http://www.aronson.com

This site offers discounts on over 1,000 titles of works in psychotherapy, alcoholism, drug abuse, cognitive therapy, and child therapy, plus the choice of one free book for each one offered.

ELECTRONIC JOURNALS

Electronic Journals and Periodicals in Psychology and Related Fields

http://www.yu.edu/ferkauf/lists/journal.htm

Here you will find an alphabetical listing of electronic journals found on the Web.

Brown University Library of Electronic Resources

http://www.brown.edu/Facilities/University_
Library/eresources/

ERIC Articles

The latest quarterly update to the *ERIC* (Educational Resources Information Center) *Digest* database features sixty-seven full-text short reports aimed at education professionals and the broader education community. Each report includes an overview of an education topic of current interest and offers references for further information. Sample titles include *Improving Ethnic and Racial Relations in the Schools, Libraries and Democracy, Social Identity and the Adult ESL Classroom,* and *A Paradigm Shift from Instruction to Learning.* Users can search the entire ERIC Digests database from the index page. ERIC, part of the National Library of Education (NLE), is a nationwide education information system sponsored by the U.S. Department of Education's Office of Educational Research and Improvement (OERI). *ERIC Digest's* Index Page is found at: **http://eric.ed.gov/.**

Sample ERIC Articles. This digest was created by ERIC, The Educational Resources Information Center. For more information about ERIC, contact ACCESS ERIC: 1-800-LET-ERIC.

ERIC Digest. "Helping Young Children Deal with Anger." Author: Marion, Marian. ERIC Clearinghouse on Elementary and Early Childhood Education. Champaign, IL. ED414077 97

Helping Children Develop Self-Regulatory Skills. Realizing that the children in their care have a very limited ability to regulate their own emotions, teachers of infants and toddlers do a lot of self-regulation "work." As children get older, adults can gradually transfer control of the self to children so that they develop self-regulatory skills.

Encouraging Children to Label Feelings of Anger. Teachers and parents can help young children produce a label for their anger by teaching them that they are having a feeling and that they can use a word to describe their angry feeling. A permanent record (a book or chart) can be made of lists of labels for anger (e.g., mad, irritated, annoyed), and the class can refer to it when discussing angry feelings.

Encouraging Children to Talk About Anger-Arousing Interactions. Preschool children better understand anger and other emotions when adults explain emotions (Denham, Zoller, and Couchoud, 1994). When children are embroiled in an anger-arousing interaction, teachers can help by listening without judging, evaluating, or ordering them to feel differently.

Using Books and Stories About Anger to Help Children Understand and Manage Anger. Well-presented stories about anger and other emotions validate children's feelings and give information about anger (Jalongo, 1986; Marion, 1995). It is important to preview all books about anger because some stories teach irresponsible anger management.

SARA

This service is provided by Carfax Publishing. Contents pages for all of the journals, for those in a subject cluster, or for just one title can be requested, all free of charge! To register for this complimentary service either:

1. Access SARA (**http://www.tandf.co.uk/sara**) and follow the on-screen instructions, or
2. Send an email to SARA@carfax.co.uk with the word "info" in the body of the message.

FIRNmail

FIRN's electronic mail (email) service features an easy to use word processing editor, online messaging, interfaces to other email systems world wide, access to limited number of Internet services, and a conferencing system which serves as a bulletin board service. The phone number for FIRN Support Staff/Help desk is (800-749-3476)

PROFESSIONAL RESOURCES

Guides to Internet Resources

http://www.clearinghouse.net

The Argus Clearinghouse offers a large collection of guides to Internet resources categorized by topic.

Federal Government Information

http://www.lib.lsu.edu/gov/fedgov.html

This is the Louisiana State University Libraries United States Federal Government Agencies Page.

Library Catalogs

http://www.libdex.com

LibDex is a directory of library catalogs which can be searched via the Web.

Library of Congress

http://catalog.loc.gov/

This site provides access to the holdings of the Library of Congress, United States Government copyright files, federal legislation, foreign law, and gateway access to many other library catalogs.

Brief Counseling That Works: A Solution-Focused Approach for School Counselors

This title can be ordered directly from the publisher:

http://www.corwinpress.com

National Network for Family Resiliency

http://www.agnr.umd.edu/nnfr/home.html

Counseling Center Village

http://ub-counseling.buffalo.edu/ccv.html

Connecting with Others: Lessons for Teaching Social and Emotional Competence

http://www.researchpress.com/scripts/
product.asp?item=4917

Volumes are available for K–2, 3–5, 6–8, and 9–12.

Community Peacemakers

http://www.compeace.org

This site, geared toward educators, is full of counseling material for classroom use. For more information about the program's organizer, Community Peacemakers, please send an email to: compeace@ concentric.net

PROFESSIONAL SERVICES

American Academy of Pediatrics

`http://www.aap.org`

This Web site is committed to the attainment of optimal physical, mental, and social health for all infants, children, adolescents, and young adults.

The American Psychiatric Association

`http://www.psych.org`

The American Psychiatric Association is a national medical specialty society whose 40,500 physician members specialize in the diagnosis and treatment of mental and emotional illnesses and substance use disorders.

American Psychological Association (APA)

`http://www.apa.org/about/division/div28.html`

This is the home page for the Division of Psychopharmacology and Substance Abuse of the American Psychological Association. Of interest to psychologists practicing in the drug abuse field may be the Web site for the APA College of Professional Psychology.

American Psychological Society (APS)

`http://www.psychologicalscience.org`

Advancing the scientific discipline and the giving away of psychology in the public interest is the aim of this site.

American Public Health Association

`http://www.apha.org`

The American Public Health Association (APHA) is the oldest and largest organization of public health professionals in the world, representing more than 50,000 members from over fifty occupations of public health. The Association and its members have been influencing policies and setting priorities in public health since 1872.

Brain Disorders Network

`http://www.brainnet.org`

The Brain Disorders Network is sponsored by the National Foundation for Brain Research.

The Centers for Disease Control and Prevention (CDC)

http://www.cdc.gov

The Centers for Disease Control and Prevention (CDC), located in Atlanta, Georgia, USA, is an agency of the Public Health Service, in the Department of Health and Human Services. Its mission is to promote health and quality of life by preventing and controlling disease, injury, and disability.

National Alliance for Hispanic Health

http://www.hispanichealth.org

Its mission is to improve the health and well-being of all Hispanic communities throughout the United States.

The Institute of Behavioral Research at TCU

http://www.ibr.tcu.edu

The Institute of Behavioral Research (IBR) at TCU conducts evaluations of drug abuse and addiction services. Special attention is given to assessing and analyzing individual functioning, treatment delivery, and engagement process, and their relationships to outcomes. Treatment improvement protocols developed and tested emphasize cognitive and behavioral strategies for programs in community-bases as well as criminal justice settings. Its people, projects, publications, and training programs are described, and a variety of data collection forms are available for downloading.

National Criminal Justice Reference Service (NCJRS)

http://www.whitehousedrugpolicy.gov
http://www.ncjrs.org/

The National Criminal Justice Reference Service (NCJRS) is one of the most extensive sources of information on criminal and juvenile justice in the world, providing services to an international community of policymakers and professionals. NCJRS is a collection of clearinghouses supporting all bureaus of the U.S. Department of Justice, Office of Justice Programs: the National Institute of Justice, the Office of Juvenile Justice and Delinquency Prevention, the Bureau of Justice Statistics, the Bureau of Justice Assistance, the Office for Victims of Crime, and the OJP Program Offices. It also supports the Office of National Drug Control Policy. National Families in Action (NFIA).

National Families in Action (NFIA)

http://www.emory.edu/NFIA

A private, nonprofit membership organization founded in 1977. It helped create and lead the parent movement, the first tier of the prevention movement that drove drug use down by two-thirds among adolescents and young adults between 1979 and 1992. Its goal is to help parents prevent drug abuse in their families and communities.

National Library of Medicine

http://www.nlm.nih.gov

The National Library of Medicine is the world's largest library dealing with a single scientific/professional topic. It cares for over 4.5 million holdings (including books, journal, reports, manuscripts, and audio-visual items).

National Board for Certified Counselors (NBCC)

http://www.nbcc.org/

This site contains listings for information on state and national credentialing, graduate student updates, bulletins, and a newsletter with NCC LINC. Also included is an RACC bulletin which contains information on summer fellowships.

Career Counseling Resources
CAREER GUIDANCE

College is Possible

http://www.CollegeIsPossible.org

Created by the Coalition of America's Colleges, this site is offered as a guide for parents and students to information and advice on higher education, especially with regard to financial matters. The site is composed of three primary sections: Preparing for College, Choosing the Right College, and Paying for College. The first section offers a ten-step guide (beginning with pre-school), recommended secondary school courses, and an electronic and print resource library.

Lynn Friedman, Ph.D.'s Web Site

http://www.drlynnfriedman.com

This site provides answers to questions about the trials and tribulations in the workplace, dealing with challenging interpersonal situations, negotiating salary, finding a better job, and establishing and pursuing life goals at work and in life.

Career Journal from the Wall Street Journal

`http://www.careerjournal.com`

A most excellent resource, this is a listing of online job databases and related tools and sites.

EXPLORE

`www.act.org/explore`

ACT's eighth grade program includes a workbook in which students develop a four year plan based on the results of the Interest Inventory, UNIACT, and the results of their achievement scores in English, math, reading, and science reasoning.

Career Counseling Netserve

`Email: cardevnet-request@world.std.com`

This site lists counseling discussion groups. From there you can click on CARDEVNET (Career Development Network Discussion List). To sign on, send the message (in the body, no subject), subscribe (no quotation marks).

VOCATIONAL EDUCATION/SCHOOL-TO-WORK

National Center for Research in Vocational Education

`http://vocserve.berkeley.edu/SkillsPage.html`

This site includes full texts of newsletters, monographs, and other reports produced by NCRVE. It also includes skill standards links, a calendar of events, and a listing of school-to-work technical assistance providers. A mini-catalogue can be found at:

New York Department of Labor

`http://www.labor.state.ny.us/`

This site focuses on youth career and has information about choosing a career, acquiring needed skills, finding a job, and tools for educators. It also has links to working papers and a career resource library.

Office of Vocational and Adult Education

http://www.ed.gov/about/offices/list/ovae/index.
html?src=mr

This site includes a variety of information about initiatives, resources, grants, technical assistance providers, research, and events.

Education Week

http://www.edweek.org/

The *Education Week* newspaper has a site containing school-to-work articles from its archives. It also provides other print and Web resources on school-to-work.

PORTFOLIOS

Federal Employment Opportunities

http://www.usajobs.opm.gov

This site contains job listing from the Veterans Administration.

HealthCareerWeb

http://www.healthcareerweb.com

This site provides services for job seekers and includes a job search feature, a resume database, and a free job-match service. The site also markets products.

America's Career InfoNet

http://www.acinet.org

This site offers registered users America's Job Bank listing of thousands of job vacancies and America's Talent Bank for employers in search of a database of resumes.

CAREER DEVELOPMENT COMPUTER SOFTWARE

COIN

http://www.coin3.com

This Guidance Program comes in both Windows and Mac platforms. It is a very complete program. COIN Educational Products, Inc, can be reached at 1-800-274-8515.

School Counseling Resources

GUIDANCE CURRICULUM

Classroom Guidance Activities

http://www.educationalmedia.com/Merchant2/
merchant.mv

Elementary School Counselors will enjoy this Sourcebook. (There is also an edition available for Secondary School Counselors.) The authors are; Joe Wittmer, Ph.D., Diane W. Thompson, Ed.S., and Larry C. Loesch, Ph.D. If you would like to order a copy of this book you can write or call the publisher at Educational Media Corporation, PO Box 21311, Minneapolis, MN 55421-0311, (612) 781-0088. The cost of the book is $24.95.

I Am Responsible

http://teacher.scholastic.com/lessonrepro/
lessonplans/theme/resp48.htm

This integrated theme unit connects classroom learning and life lessons.

We Are Family

http://teacher.scholastic.com/lessonrepro/
lessonplans/theme/fam23.htm

This integrated theme unit explores all kinds of families. You can choose from Kindergarten through grade 1, grades 2 to 3, and grades 4 to 8.

Bibliotherapy in Elementary Schools

http://reading.indiana.edu/

This is a useful site for conducting bibliocounseling with elementary students.

Susquehanna Institute

http://www.susquehanna-institute.com

Help support free and low-cost counseling by ordering books, CDs, videos, and games.

Access Eric

http://www.eric.ed.gov

This is the gateway to the Internet sites of the Educational Resources Information Center (ERIC).

A Tour of the World Wide Web for School Counselors

http://www.thejournal.com/articles/13972

World School Directory

http://www.education-world.com/regional/k12_schools

This site is a country-by-country and state-by-state guide to K12 Schools, Universities, and Education Resources around the world. Users can find the following LOCAL Schools within this guide:

• Charter Schools & School Districts
• Montessori Schools
• Parochial Schools & School Districts
• Private Schools
• Public Schools & School Districts
• Gifted and Talented School Districts
• Special Needs School Districts
• Universities & University Departments

Also available are the following related resources:

• Education Organizations
• K12 School Libraries
• School Newspapers
• K12 School Publications
• Alumni Publications
• Regional Education Resources
• Vocational—Technical Schools
• Gifted and Talented School
• International School
• Magnet Schools
• Online Schools
• Special Needs Schools

Goals 2000

http://www.ed.gov/pubs/G2KReforming

Goals 2000: Reforming Education to Improve Student Achievement (April 1998) looks at how Goals 2000 supports state efforts to develop clear and rigorous standards for what every child should know and be able to do, and supports comprehensive state- and district-wide planning and implementation of school efforts focused on improving student achievement of those standards.

ASCD Education Bulletin

Email: Bulletin@listserv.ascd.org

This biweekly online newsletter of the Association for Supervision and Curriculum Development (ASCD) International is dedicated to sharing and exchanging information on the issues of international development, democracy, and professional development.

American School Counselors Association Materials

http://www.schoolcounselor.org

ASCA has also developed national standards for school counselors. Descriptions of the duties and goals of school counselors are listed. Copies are available on their Web site along with *Get a Life Portfolio* (in single or bulk rates):

- *Facilitator's Manual*—eight chapters of practical information and inservice activities for local staff and community helpers (131 pages).
- *Facilitator's Guide*—5-page quick-reference guide to help teachers and advisors maximize the *Get A Life Portfolio.*
- *Introductory Video* (10 minutes)—introduces the program to school staff, parents, and community groups.
- *Get A Life Software*—storage, retrieval, and editing software to help track student goals (DOS compatible, 3-½" disks).
- *Macintosh Programming Guide*—for customizing the program and creating word processing files on a Macintosh computer.

Transitioning

http://www.middleweb.com/INCASE5to6.html

A collection of good ideas for fifth–sixth grade transitioning.

Transition and Continuity between Head Start and Public Schools

http://www.psy.miami.edu/faculty/dgreenfield/research

This site includes benefits of transition, keys to successful transition key concepts about transition to kindergarten, a transition checklist, differences between early childhood and kindergarten, and a kindergarten observer's worksheet.

Behavioral Interventions

Email: vstanhope@naspweb.org

The newly released publication from the Center, *Behavioral Interventions: Creating a Safe Environment in Our Schools* discusses behavioral problems in children, highlighting positive strategies and interventions. To request a free copy of *Behavioral Interventions,* email Victoria Stanhope at vstanhope@naspweb.org and give your regular mailing address.

Communities That Care

http://www.cisnet.org
http://www.americaspromise.org

For information on how to become one of Colin Powell's Schools of Promise, visit this Web site or that of Communities in Schools.

Learning Style Inventory

http://www.howtolearn.com/personal.html

Twenty-four item learning style online survey. An evaluation tool to assess learning styles. Identifies visual/auditory/tactile learners and gives a description of each style.

K–12 Practitioners Home Page—NCES

http://nces.ed.gov/practitioners

The National Center for Education Statistics (NCES) has launched a site for K–12 practitioners that summarizes and explains some of the latest educational research findings. Survey data that support these findings, as well as methods used to conduct the surveys are outlined. Teachers, administrators, school support staff, and parents can examine articles in the Research Findings section on topics such as Teacher Job Satisfaction, At-Risk Students, and the Pipeline to Higher Education. Links to additional NCES resources and organizations affiliated with NCES projects are also included.

Idea Book

http://www.ed.gov/pubs/Idea_Planning

Implementing Schoolwide Programs: An Idea Book on Planning presents methods and resources for planning schoolwide programs and for measuring their success. It also focuses on the fact that school-wide programs have the flexibility to combine many federal education funds with state and local funds to operate. Featured are schools that have a record of improving student performance; cohesive planning; a comprehensive, standards-based curriculum; highly qualified staff who are committed to building a culture of learning; family, school, and community partnerships that have helped sustain the school's academic achievements and have combined Title I funds with state and local resources.

Education World®

http://www.education-world.com

This site where educators go to learn is a database of over 110,000 sites featuring what's new, education topics, guide site reviews, world resource center, world school directory, cool schools, employment listings, events calendar, distribution lists, message boards, questionnaire, and awards and accolades.

7 Habits

http://www.usaweekend.com/99_issues/990124/
990124coveyhour.html

Let the 7 Habits author and USA Weekend contributing editor show you how to better realize life goals with quizzes and articles at the Stephen Covey Archive.

School Psychology Resource Online

http://www.schoolpsychology.net

This is an online resource for the school psychology community. Information on learning disabilities, ADHD, gifted, autism, adolescence, parenting, and assessment are just a few of the many resources offered.

Consortium for School Networking (CoSN)

http://www.cosn.org

Certified Cognitive-Behavioral School Counselor

http://www.nacbt.org

For a grandfathering application, call 1-800-853-1135 or email with your name and street address to nacbt@nacbt.org.

Icebreakers and Energizers

`http://www.kimskorner4teachertalk.com/`
`classmanagement/icebreakers.html`

This site includes some of the traditional ideas such as "people bingo" but has others as well.

Teaching Young Children How to Visualize

`ASCD Education Bulletin`

The biweekly online newsletter of the Association for Supervision and Curriculum Development. To subscribe:

Email:
To: BULLETIN@LISTSERV.ASCD.ORG
Subject: ASCD Education Bulletin

Nicenet

`http://www.nicenet.org`

Nicenet is a way for educators to set up a Web page without having to format anything. Type in the information. Try setting up a temporary account so you can view its features.

Teacher/Advisor Site

`http://www.mentors.ca`

This site includes an annotated bibliography that is searchable and contains virtually every published article about the Teacher–Advisor system. Seminars are provided on establishing such systems, and the Web site includes details about that curriculum as well.

Peer Counseling/Mentoring/Helping Sites

`http://www.islandnet.com/~rcarr`
`http://www.peerhelping.org`

School Psychology Resources Online

`http://www.schoolpsychology.net`

WCN (Interactive Counseling Community)

`http://www.CounselingNetwork.com`

COUNSELING SPECIAL CLIENT POPULATIONS

Annotated Guide to a Parent's Research for Gifted Children

http://www.stephanietolan.com/is_it_a_cheetah.htm

Is It A Cheetah? by Stephanie Tolan. This essay uses the analogy of identifying, classifying, and caging a cheetah to address some of the problems associated with raising, teaching, or being a gifted child. Good light reading.

http://www.gifteddevelopment.com/What_is_Gifted/
learned.htm

What We Have Learned About Gifted Children, by Linda Silverman. Key findings indicate that gifted children need different teaching methods from non-gifted learners, and that gifted children have better social adjustment in classes with children like themselves, whether age-peer gifted or intellectual peers.

http://www.gt-cybersource.org/Record.aspx?NavID=
2_0&rid=13348

The Miseducation of Our Gifted Children, by Ellen Winner, in *Education Week.* Providing special education to gifted children offends our egalitarian sensibilities, but we need to recognize the importance of appropriate education techniques to teaching gifted children.

http://www.hoagiesgifted.org/struggle.htm

Struggle, Challenge, and Meaning: The Education of a Gifted Child, by Valerie Bock. Gifted children deserve the same opportunities as other children to test their mettle and emerge victorious, and to experience the rewards of meaningful work.

http://www.hoagiesgifted.org/enrichment.htm

Horizontal Enrichment versus Vertical Acceleration, by Draper Kauffman, Ed.D. Items with standard 2nd grade vocabulary and standard explanations are unlikely to interest a gifted 2nd grader.

http://www.hoagiesgifted.org/wish_list.htm

Parents Wish List for Educators, Jean Schweers, Ed.D. "We, the parents of gifted and talented students, wish schools, administrators, and teachers would. . . ."

Hoagies' Gifted Education Page

http://www.hoagiesgifted.org/

This extensive site helps meet the needs of parents and educators of gifted children. Included are articles, research, books, organizations, conferences, online support groups, academic programs, products, and organizations that support gifted education locally, nationally, and globally.

Selective Mutism

http://www.anxietynetwork.com/spsm.html

Anxiety Disorders Association of America

http://www.adaa.org

Association for the Advancement of Behavior Therapy

http://www.aabt.org

Selective Mutism Foundation

http://www.selectivemutismfoundation.org/

Suite 101: Special Education Site

http://www.suite101.com/welcome.cfm/special_ education

This site rates the top five Web sites for special education. It also contains current featured articles and links for parents with children in special education.

American Association of Mental Retardation

http://www.aamr.org

This is an online resource for publications, training, careers, conventions, policies, and resources.

Bureau for At Risk Youth

http://www.at-risk.com

This is a resource site to help today's youth cope with important issues that face them. It includes an at risk resources directory, an issues forum, a buyer's guide, and a free catalogue order form.

ADHD/ADD Regulation Site

http://www.ed.gov/offices/OSERS/IDEA/Brief-6.html

This is a Web site that offers access to federal regulations online via GPO access. It contains a browse feature and also contains final regulations on Brief 6 for children with ADD/ADHD—March 1999.

ADD Assessment

http://www.amenclinic.com.

Dr. Daniel Amen has a fascinating Web site that has a huge source of resources related to ADD/ADHD. One of his books, *Windows Into the ADD Mind,* is great reading for someone interested in the subject.

Children and Adults with Attention Deficit Disorder (CHADD)

http://www.chadd.org

ADD Newsletter

http://www.helpforadd.com

In addition to this site, David Rabiner also publishes an online newsletter entitled *ADHD research update.* There is a modest cost for the online research newsletter however David offers free issues for review.

ADD Main Table of Contents

http://www3.sympatico.ca/frankk/contents.html

Fifty Tips on the Classroom Management of Attention Deficit Disorder

http://www3.sympatico.ca/frankk/50class.html

LD in Depth: ADD/ADHD Resources

http://www.ldonline.org/ld_indepth/add_adhd/add-adhd.html

National Attention Deficit Disorder Association

http://www.add.org/

ADD Warehouse

`http://www.addwarehouse.com`

1-800-233-9273

ADHD/Special Needs Resources: Kids Who Thrive "Outside the Box!"

`http://adhd.kids.tripod.com`

Grade Level: K–12, Parent & Professional

Adults with Attention Deficit Disorder

`Email: adult@maelstrom.stjohns.edu`

http://yourhealthdaily.com	Daily Health News
http://school.discovery.com/ homeworkhelp/bjpinchbeck	Outstanding Kid's Resource Page
http://www.nfgcc.org	(National Foundation for Gifted and Creative Children)
http://www.studentservices.com/ fastweb/	Financial Aid Scholarship Search

ACT Web Site—Information for Life's Transitions

`http://www.act.org`

Closed Captioning Web

`http://www.captions.org`

This site has information accessible to students with hearing impairments, ESL, and other language difficulties. Links to companies that provide nonprofessional captioning software are available so that, for a relatively small fee, counselors can caption their own educational materials.

Disability Information and Resources

`http://www.makoa.org`

A directory of many disability resources. This site contains links to general disability resources, newsletters, Web sites on people with disabilities, a disability-solutions page, and current political stances of disability.

Dyslexia

http://www.dyslexia.com

The Gift is an online information center dedicated to the positive side of learning disability as well as to remedial therapies and teaching methods suited to the dyslexic learning style.

Internet Resources for Special Children

http://www.irsc.org

Information for parents, educators, medical professionals, and others who interact with children who have disabilities.

MedWeb

http://www.medweb.emory.edu/medweb/default.htm

Contains links to an array of disability-related information.

Organizations and Associations Worldwide for Down Syndrome

http://www.nas.com/downsyn/org.html

Includes contact information and links, when available, to worldwide associations for Down Syndrome.

Pregnancy & Parenting iVillage

http://parenting.ivillage.com/

Pregnancy & Parenting iVillage is a parenting library about learning disabilities and dyslexia. It contains articles ranging from memory problems to treatment.

Recording for the Blind and Dyslexic (RFB&D)

http://www.rfbd.org

A national nonprofit organization that serves people who cannot read standard print because of a visual, perceptual, or other physical disability. The organization also offers the nonprofit sale of dictionaries, reference materials, and professional books on computer disk (E-text), and specially adapted tape players/recorders to use with their audio books.

The Sibling Support Project Home Page

http://www.thearc.org/siblingsupport/

Dedicated to the interests of brothers and sisters of people with special health and developmental needs, this site offers information about workshops, existing sibling programs, resources, and SibNet (a list service for siblings of people with special needs.

National Academy for Child Development (NACD)

http://www.nacd.org

An international organization of parents and professionals dedicated to helping children and adults reach their full potential, NACD designs very specific home educational and therapeutic programs for infants, children, and adults.

The James Stanfield Publishing Company

http://www.stanfield.com

The most respected library of educational materials available today for students with cognitive challenges, the company provides texts for programs about assertion training, sexuality education, social skills, and working skills.

UPSIDE!

http://www.telebyte.com/upside/upside.html

National Organization of Rare Disorders, Inc. (NORD)

http://www.rarediseases.org

NORD is a federation of more than 140 not-for-profit volunteer health organizations serving people with rare disorders and disabilities.

Kids Together, Inc.

http://www.kidstogether.org

The mission statement of this nonprofit organization is "To promote inclusive communities where all people belong." The site provides helpful information and resources to enhance the quality of life for children and adults with disabilities, and for communities. Businesses can take advantage of the numerous marketing opportunities offered by the Kids Together Day Festival.

Healthy Oakland Teens Curriculum

`http://www.caps.ucsf.edu/curricula/hotcurr.html`

The Healthy Oakland Teens curriculum is divided into six teacher-led sessions and eight peer-led sessions available for download.

ASSESSMENT AND TESTING RESOURCES

Consulting Psychologists Press, Inc.

`http://www.cpp-db.com/`

CPP is the exclusive publisher of the Myers-Briggs Type Indicator. (MBTI), Strong Interest InventoryTM, FIROTM, and the CPITM.

Keirsey Temperament and Character Web Site

`http://www.keirsey.com`

This link is for a free test that is very similar to the Myers-Briggs.

Buros Institute of Mental Measurements

`http://www.unl.edu/buros`

This site provides professional assistance, expertise, and information to users of commercially published tests. Listed are records of over 10,000 tests and research instruments, including information about ETS tests on microfiche. The site includes a test locator and subject index.

ERIC/AE Test Locator

`http://buros.unl.edu/buros/jsp/search.jsp`

This is an updated test locator including ERIC Clearinghouse for assessment and evaluation.

PARENT EDUCATION

American Library Association's site

`http://www.ala.org/parentspage`

Family Education Network

`http://familyeducation.com/article/0,1120,1-9834-1,00.html`

Apple Learning Interchange

http://www.apple.com/education/community/ali.html

These online handouts contain wonderful topics such as how to complain constructively, the importance of reading, parent and family places online, parents, homework, and computers, preparing your child for the first day of school, and separation anxieties.

PARENTING WORKSHOPS

The Positive Parenting Page

http://positiveparenting.com/

Stephen Glenn and Jane Nelsen's work

http://www.empoweringpeople.com

Step Kit by Dinkmeyer

http://www.agsnet.com

The National PTA

http://www.pta.org

The National PTA has developed national standards for parent and family involvement in schools.

The Connect for Kids Weekly

http://www.connectforkids.org

This site is a source for the latest news on issues affecting kids and families published by the Benton Foundation.

Red Ribbon Week Resource

http://www.redribboncoalition.org

Home and School Institute

http://www.MegaSkillsHSI.org

How do parents rate the teachers of their children? What can schools and teachers learn from parents' answers to questions like "Does this teacher appear to enjoy teaching and believe in what he or she does in school"? Dorothy Rich of the Home and School Institute explores the results of such surveys in her EL article, *What Parents Want from Teachers.*

MEDIATION RESOURCES/SAFE SCHOOLS

Conflict Resolution

http://www.bouldenpublishing.com

This site offers free demo conflict resolution interactive CDs to elementary school counselors. This CD runs on both Mac and PC and contains relaxation exercise plus limited demo of interactive material. If interested, send $3.75 to cover shipping to address below. email: jboulden@bouldenpub.com

NCES Publication Released

http://nces.ed.gov/pubsearch

This report, *Indicators of School Crime and Safety, 1988,* is the first in a series of annual reports on school crime and safety from the Bureau of Justice Statistics and the National Center for Education Statistics. It presents the latest available data on school crime and student safety. The report provides a profile of school crime and safety in the United States and describes the characteristics of the victims of these crimes. It is organized as a series of indicators, with each indicator presenting data on different aspects of school crime and safety. There are five sections to the report: Nonfatal Student Victimization—Student Reports; Violence and Crime at School; Nonfatal Teacher Victimization at School—Teacher Reports; and School Environment. Each section contains a set of indicators that, taken as a whole, describe a distinct aspect of school crime and safety.

Center for Prevention of School Violence

http://www.ncdjjdp.org/cpsv/

This site offers information, program assistance, and research on school violence prevention. The "Safe Schools Pyramid" offers prevention programs such as "School Resource Officers" and "Conflict Management Peer Mediation."

NEA Today Online: One Year After the School Shootings

http://www.nea.org/neatoday

In the year since the tragic school shootings in Arkansas, Oregon, and Pennsylvania, NEA members nationwide have been working to create schools where all students feel safe. The April edition of *NEA Today Online* synthesizes the latest research.

NEA Response to Littleton, Colorado

http://www.nea.org/nr/st990421.html

This NEA html page posts responses and recommendations for prevention of school violence after the Littleton, Colorado massacre.

Blueprint for Violence Prevention

http://www.colorado.edu/cspv/blueprints/index.html

This site is an excellent resource for violence prevention from the Center for the Study and Prevention of Violence (CSPV) and the Colorado Division of Criminal Justice and the Center for Disease Control (CDC). This site identifies ten violence prevention programs which meet high standards in program effectiveness. They include: Midwestern Prevention, Big Brothers—Big Sisters, Functional Family Therapy, Multisystemic Therapy, Nursing Home Visitation, Treatment Foster Care, Quantum Opportunities, Life Skills Training, Paths, and Bullying Prevention.

HOMESCHOOLING

Homeschool Headlines

http://www.homeschoolheadlines.com

A free online publication to support, inform, and empower homeschoolers, this site offers many articles. Some articles offer practical advice about teaching math; others tell success stories. Click on "Controversial Issues" for differing views on the questions: Should There Be a Separation Between School and State? or Should Government Continue Directing Education in America? The site also includes newsletters aimed at homeschoolers in Maryland and Pennsylvania.

Colleges That Admit Homeschoolers FAQ

http://learninfreedom.org/colleges_4_hmsc.html

Here's another page from "School Is Dead; Learn in Freedom!" You've homeschooled your kids and now it's time to think about applying to college. This site lists more than 730 links to colleges and universities that have accepted homeschooled students. Scroll through the list to find information and resources from universities, homeschooling associations, and government agencies.

The National Homeschool Association

http://www.n-h-a.org

Based in the United States, this association's site isn't very interactive, but it provides basic information about the association's mission, philosophy, and offerings. An address and telephone number are listed for further details.

Calvert School

http://home.calvertschool.org

An accredited home instruction source long used by United States foreign service personnel, missionaries, and other folks stationed in remote places, this nonprofit organization offers a full nondenominational, nonsectarian curriculum for K–8 students, including advisory teachers, chat rooms, electronic bulletin boards, CD-ROMs, and multimedia resources.

Christian Homeschooling

http://www.classicalhomeschooling.org

By far, the most prominent feature of homeschooling Web sites researched is the Christian faith.

Rescue 2010

http://www.nace-cee.org/rescue2010.htm

Rescue 2010 is a movement that endorses homeschooling for Christian families and promotes seeking "common ground" on controversial issues; seeking "safe-passage" for all K–12 children throughout the system by being spiritually and morally unharmed or academically stunted; and organizing Christians in every school district to become involved in their local schools to oversee and ensure the above objectives.

Islamic Educational and Muslim Home School Resources

http://www.muslimhomeschool.com

Not just the Christian faith is represented in the homeschooling community. This page offers teaching ideas for Muslims and non-

Muslims, lists curriculum resources, and sponsors a listserv for all Muslim educators.

SCHOOL COUNSELING JOURNALS

The Journal of Technology in Counseling

http://jtc.colstate.edu

A peer reviewed journal, soon to be published quarterly (July, October, January, and April) through the efforts of the Department of Counseling and Clinical Programs at Columbus State University. JTC is published in a Web-based format and represents an innovative approach to publication not seen in the counseling literature. Submissions will be accepted effective April 1, 1999. *The Journal of Technology in Counseling* publishes articles on all aspects of practice, theory, research, and professionalism related to the use of technology in counselor training and counseling practice. For more information about the journal take a look at the JTC Web site which contains a list of current journal editors, guidelines for authors, and a sample design format to assist authors.

Journal of Special Education Technology

http://jset.unlv.edu

AIDS Education and Prevention

http://www.guilford.com/periodicals/jnai.htm

Journal of HIV/AIDS Prevention and Education for Adolescents and Children

http://www.haworthpressinc.com

Addictions/Dual Diagnosis

SUBSTANCE ABUSE

Substance Abuse and Treatment of State and Federal Prisoners

http://www.ojp.usdoj.gov/bjs/abstract/satsfp97.htm

Released on January 5, this new study by the Bureau of Justice Statistics (BJS) reports a rise in the proportion of state inmates who used drugs (including alcohol) in the month before their arrest and an increase in the use by federal inmates within prisons between

1990 and 1997. In the same period, the proportions of state inmates receiving drug abuse treatment fell from 24.5 percent in 1991 to 9.7 percent in 1997, and the numbers of inmates in treatment in federal prisons fell from 15.7 percent to 9.2 percent. Analysts attribute these figures to both a new awareness by police and the court system toward offender drug use and the exploding prison population, which has doubled since it reached 1.8 million in 1981. Available in .pdf or ASCII format, the report contains data tables on "prior alcohol and drug abuse by types of offender characteristics," as well as the types of treatment and programs in prisons. A press release, spreadsheets in .zip format, and related data sets are also available.

College on Problems of Drug Dependence (CPDD)

http://views.vcu.edu/cpdd

CPDD serves as an interface among governmental, industrial, and academic communities maintaining liaisons with regulatory and research agencies as well as educational, treatment, and prevention facilities in the drug abuse field. It also functions as a collaborating center of the World Health Organization.

Drug Strategies

http://www.drugstrategies.org

Drug Strategies is a nonprofit research institute promoting more effective approaches to the nation's drug problems by supporting private and public initiatives that reduce the demand for drugs through prevention, education, treatment, law enforcement, and community coalitions.

Center for Education and Drug Abuse Research (CEDAR)

http://cedar.pharmacy.pitt.edu

CEDAR serves to elucidate the factors contributing to the variation in the liability to drug abuse and determine the developmental pathways culminating in drug abuse outcome, normal outcome, and psychiatric/behavioral disorder outcome. CEDAR is a consortium between the University of Pittsburgh and St. Francis Medical Center.

Drug and Alcohol Treatment Prevention Services

http://www.phoenixhouse.org/

This site contains information on drugs and other harmful substances and contains a database of more then 1,200 treatment programs. It also covers topics like alcohol in the workplace, drugs and pregnancy, and talking to a child about marijuana.

International Narcotics Research Conference (INRC)

http://www.inrcworld.org

The International Narcotics Research Conference is an annual meeting designed to bring together drug abuse researchers from around the world. A diverse group of scientists present their latest results on the basic mechanisms of narcotic drug action. Important advances in molecular, cellular, and behavioral aspects of narcotic action are presented and discussed. Attendance is open and further information can be obtained from:

The National Center on Addiction and Substance Abuse at Columbia University (CASA)

http://www.casacolumbia.org

The National Center on Addiction and Substance Abuse at Columbia University (CASA) is a resource for research on addiction and substance abuse. It provides access to information, research, and commentary on tobacco, alcohol, and drug abuse issues including prevention, treatment, and cost data.

National Clearinghouse for Drug and Alcohol Information/ Prevention Online

http://www.health.org

The National Clearinghouse for Alcohol and Drug Information (NCADI) is the information service of the Center for Substance Abuse Prevention of the U.S. Department of Health and Human Services. NCADI is the world's largest resource for current information and materials about alcohol and other drugs. The National Clearinghouse for Alcohol and Drug Information is a site which contains: missing children links, funding opportunities, treatment organizations, information on federal workplace, drug testing programs, laboratories for urine drug testing, resource for runaways, Internet links, and publications from NCADI. This Web site contains links to other Internet sites related to substance abuse information.

National Association of Alcoholism and Drug Abuse Counselors

http://www.naadac.org

NAADAC's mission is to provide leadership in the alcoholism and drug abuse counseling profession by building new visions, effecting change in public policy, promoting criteria for effective treatment, encouraging adherence to ethical standards, and ensuring professional growth for alcoholism and drug abuse counselors.

The Office of National Drug Control Policy

http://www.ncjrs.org/htm/toc.htm

The Office of National Drug Control Policy (ONDCP) was established by Act of Congress in 1988 and is organized within the Executive Office of the President. ONDCP is authorized to develop and coordinate the policies, goals, and objectives of the nation's drug control program for reducing the use of illicit drugs. ONDCP engages in activities that both meet the requirements of its authorization and represent the values and commitments of the President and its Director.

The Substance Abuse and Mental Health Data Archive (SAMHDA)

http://www.icpsr.umich.edu/SAMHDA

SAMHDA's purpose is to increase the utilization of substance abuse and mental health databases, thereby encouraging their use to understand and assess the extent of alcohol, drug abuse, and mental health disorders, and the nature and impact of related treatment systems. Based at the University of Michigan's Inter-university Consortium for Political and Social Research (ICPSR).

Web of Addictions

http://www.well.com/user/woa

The Web of Addictions is dedicated to providing accurate information about alcohol and other drug addictions. The Web of Addictions was developed for several reasons: concern about the pro drug use messages in some Web sites and in some use groups; concern about the appalling extent of misinformation about abused drugs on the Internet, particularly on some usenet news groups; and the desire to provide a resource for teachers, students, and others who need factual information about abused drugs.

National Institute on Drug Abuse (NIDA)

http://www.nida.nih.gov

This Web site contains recent studies funded by NIDA, research on tobacco, research on economic costs of alcohol and drug abuse in the United States, latest survey results, research reports on addiction, NIDA information fax, a bi-monthly newsletter, materials for teachers, scientists, health practitioners, and students, subscription to mailing lists, science drug education, constituent organizations, grantees, government sites of interest, and site searches.

http://www.nida.nih.gov/Prevention/Prevopen.html

The government has officially embraced a new approach to drug abuse, emphasizing both counseling and medical treatment of addiction. The National Institute on Drug Abuse issued two treatment manuals that take counselors and other professionals step-by-step through a drug treatment program. "For the first time the strategy is what I feel to be a science-based strategy," NIDA director Dr. Alan Leshner told a conference of drug abuse professionals.

Children of Alcoholics

http://www.hazelden.org

Collegiate Alcohol and Other Drug Use

http://www.robertchapman.net/

Center for Education and Drug Abuse Research (University of Pittsburgh)

http://cedar.pharmacy.pitt.edu

Phoenix House

http://www.phoenixhouse.org

This New York nonprofit substance abuse service organization has established a site with referral information, its treatment philosophy and other material.

Mental Health Net

http://mentalhelp.net/

Hope and Healing Web Chronicles

http://www.hopeandhealing.com/

Hope and Healing Web Chronicles is a healing journal focusing on the spiritual journeys and personal transformations possible for the family affected by alcoholism and addiction. The site includes insights, observations and musings of the Web publisher, W. Waldo; articles by well-known published authors; and numerous links and descriptions of Web sites related to alcoholism. This extensive site is a great place to look for support for alcoholism.

Twelve Step Cyber Cafe

http://www.12steps.org/

The goal of this site is to help visitors find information about addiction, as well as the help that is available. Visitors that are new to recovery might find the Menuboard of Recovery helpful. This site provides a chat room for its visitors to share their experiences with each other, and a bulletin board which provides some helpful information on local meetings throughout the world. This site is frequently updated and simple to navigate.

Christians in Recovery

http://www.christians-in-recovery.com

Members work to regain and maintain balance and order in their lives through active discussion of the Twelve Steps, the Bible, and experiences in their own recovery. The only purpose of Christians in Recovery is to provide information and referral for anyone who desires to recover from abuse, family dysfunction, addictions of alcohol, drugs, food, and pornography. Christians in Recovery does not engage in providing individualized professional services or counseling.

Recovery Online

http://www.usdrugrehabcenters.com/

A comprehensive listing of self-help, recovery groups online, including twelve-step groups, religious groups, as well as secular groups. This is a great place to begin a search!

Al-Anon/Alateen

http://www.Al-Anon-Alateen.org

Al-Anon (and Alateen for younger members) is a worldwide organization that offers a self-help recovery program for families and friends of alcoholics. The listings of the Twelve Steps, Traditions, and Concepts of Al-Anon are helpful for those who are seeking more information on the goals and objectives of this program. Also included are an approved literature section, a discussion forum, and a guide for professionals.

Alcoholics Victorious

`http://av.iugm.org/`

A Christian oriented twelve-step support group for recovering alcoholics, the site includes information and referrals, literature, phone support, conferences, support group meetings, and the organization's newsletter. An informative FAQ is provided for new visitors.

Big Book of Alcoholics Anonymous

`http://www.recovery.org/aa/bigbook/ww/`

An indexed and fully searchable copy of the main text of Alcoholics Anonymous. Also online is the unpublished, original manuscript of the book.

Connecticut Clearinghouse

`http://www.ctclearinghouse.org/`

Connecticut Clearinghouse is a resource center for information about alcohol, tobacco, and other drugs. A fact sheet answers many common questions in a easy-to-read manner, the research page keeps you up-to-date on certain projects, and the message page allows one to interact with others. The Connecticut Clearinghouse provides free information to Connecticut residents about chemical dependency and related topics such as mental illness, violence, fetal alcohol syndrome, and suicide.

Kathleen Sciacca

`http://www.erols.com/ksciacca/`

This site is designed to provide information and resources for service providers, consumers, and family members who are seeking assistance and/or education in the field of co-occurring mental illness, drug addiction and/or alcoholism in various combinations.

HabitSmart

`http://www.habitsmart.com/`

This Web site has been constructed to provide an abundance of information about addictive behavior, including theories of habit endurance and habit change as well as tips for effectively managing problematic habitual behavior. Includes the Self-Scoring Alcohol Check-Up, an online questionnaire for people concerned about their alcohol consumption. Many of the articles are written by Robert W. Westermeyer, Ph.D.

Indiana Prevention Resource Center

http://www.drugs.indiana.edu/

An information clearinghouse of prevention, technical assistance, and information about alcohol, tobacco, and other drugs. This site includes searchable databases (including an online dictionary of street drug slang), more than 1,000 full-text documents, more than 2,000 links to prevention sites and Web pages, and a library of more than 200 educational photos of drugs available for free download. Although this site provides a great deal of information, it is not regularly updated.

National Association for Christian Recovery

http://www.nacronline.com

Especially helpful for clients struggling with spiritual or faith-related issues that complicate recovery, this site contains many articles, meditations, forums, and other resources, and is frequently updated.

Arizona Smokers Helpline

http://www.ashline.org

A very large resource for smoking and tobacco related links. This site's library of links is divided up into 8 categories and provides many choices within each. We found it fairly easy to use, but it lacks its own content on tobacco and related topics.

LifeRing: Because People in Recovery Deserve a Choice

http://www.unhooked.com/

The Secular Organizations for Sobriety (SOS) is an alternative, recovery method for those alcoholics or drug addicts who are uncomfortable with the spiritual content of widely available twelve-step programs. It is a rich resource, but the home page is very busy with navigation options and graphics. A helpful FAQ answers questions in a direct manner about the organization and what it's all about.

SMART Recovery

http://www.smartrecovery.org/

SMART Recovery is an abstinence-based, not-for-profit organization with a self-help program for people having problems with drinking and using. This frequently updated site provides a broad overview of what the organization is about. It also contains several primers and manuals concerning alcoholism.

Sobriety and Recovery Resources

http://www.recoveryresources.org

Loading time is lengthy for this huge list of resources for every aspect of recovery. Resources are organized for easy navigation.

Gift of Serenity

http://www.laserbuddy.com/recover/

An Al-Anon member's personal story, this site contains touching and inspiring sections on "Acceptance, Courage, Wisdom, and Hope." An excellent resource for those who are recovering from the effects of someone else's drinking problem, this site lists links to other related sites.

Close to Home Online

http://www.thirteen.org/closetohome/

This Web companion to the PBS program "Moyers on Addiction: Close to Home" offers more than just a synopsis of the TV series. You can find information about the effects of illegal drugs, a debate among experts about drug-related issues, advice, and listings of resources to combat illegal drug use. This site also features Overboard, a thirteen-issue soap opera comic book directed at teenagers.

AlcoWeb

http://www.alcoweb.com/

An informative site for laypeople as well as professionals, AlcoWeb's highlights include a glossary, prevention and health information, and related resources. Text is available in French and English.

Dual Recovery Anonymous Twelve-Step Program

http://draonline.org/

This site is very comprehensive, containing twenty-one pages. Their home page and Preamble page explain DRA's purposes, values, and philosophy. Additional pages describe their twelve steps; their twelve traditions; answer frequently asked questions; describe their meeting formats; and list where their groups are currently located. The site also includes a discussion forum page, a chat room, and a page set up to conduct an online meeting. The site also includes a recovery gift shop, links to three bookstores, and search pages, for both links to other recovery sites, and other links. Their newsletter is also available through this site. Unique links include a page linking the user to various games, and a jukebox.

Do It Now Foundation

http://www.doitnow.org/

America's drug information connection, this foundation has been developing innovative publications and education materials on substance abuse, alcoholism & related health since 1968. Currently their site archives the entire roster of educational publications in these areas. It is especially comprehensive in detailing resources about "street" drugs.

ADULT CHILDREN OF ALCOHOLICS INFORMATION

Recovery.org

http://www.recovery.org/acoa/acoa.html

This site gives very basic information on adult children of alcoholics. This resource is limited, but it might be of use to point adult children of alcoholics in the right direction.

Cocaine Anonymous

http://www.ca.org/

A fellowship of men and women who share their experience, strength and hope with each other so that they may solve their common problem and help others to recover from their addiction. The only requirement for membership is a desire to stop using cocaine and all other mind-altering substances. There are no dues or fees for membership.

Instituto para el Estudio de las Adicciones

http://www.lasdrogas.info/index.php

The Instituto para el Estudio de las Adicciones is an NGO located in Spain. It is the first Spanish Web site designed to prevent drug addiction. Visitors can find information about drugs, how to talk with children, a calendar of events, who is who, HIV, and more. All text is in Spanish. Loading time is lengthy.

Jewish Alcoholics, Chemically Dependent Persons and Significant Others

http://www.jacsweb.org/

An Internet recovery resource site for Jews and their families whose lives have been affected by alcohol and drugs. The site lists retreats (mostly based in the NYC area), and provides links to local support groups. Other resources are planned for this easy to navigate site.

Marijuana Anonymous

http://www.marijuana-anonymous.org/

Marijuana Anonymous is a fellowship of men and women who share the same experience of addiction. The only requirement for membership is a desire to stop using marijuana. This site contains membership information and pamphlets.

Minnesota Recovery Page

http://www.lakeweb1.com/mrp/

This site provides contact information for various twelve-step groups and recovery resources. An AA meeting directory for much of Minnesota is included.

Moderation Management

http://www.moderation.org/

A recovery program and national support group network for people who have made the healthy decision to reduce their drinking and make other positive lifestyle changes. Provides membership information, a national list of MM support groups, an MM mailing list, chat, and related literature for sale.

Narcotics Anonymous

`http://www.wsoinc.com/`

Provides some basic information about the Fellowship of Narcotics Anonymous. This site can be helpful in contacting with NA in or near your community.

Recovery Resources

`http://www.naturesgift.com/recov.htm`

This site contains many Al-Anon, AA, and other twelve-step resources. The author is in the process of recovery, and has created this site as an attempt to give back some of what she has been given. Broken images become distracting.

Women for Sobriety, Inc.

`http://www.womenforsobriety.org`

Women for Sobriety, Inc. (WFS) is a nonprofit organization dedicated to helping women overcome alcoholism and other addictions. The New Life program helps achieve sobriety and sustain ongoing recovery. A broad overview of the organization is provided, including special reports on the 1997 WFS Conference, WFS Group info, and the WFS bookstore.

Addiction Resource Guide

`http://www.addictionresourceguide.com`

Addiction Resource Guide is an online directory of inpatient and outpatient treatment facilities. The site has included information about addictions and how the layperson or professional can find the appropriate treatment options. To make navigation easier, resources are divided into appropriate categories. A brief description is provided for each resource listed.

Recoveries Anonymous

`http://www.r-a.org/`

The author shares his personal experience of recovery. He includes information on all aspects of addictions and how these addictions interact. The inconsistent layout interferes with navigation.

Recovery Poetry Spa

`http://www.geocities.com/HotSprings/Spa/1416/`

This site features poetry about abuse, addictions, and recovery from them. It invites additional submissions from others. Additional links to recovery and general poetry sites are included.

National Association of Addiction Treatment Providers

`http://www.naatp.org/`

National Association of Addiction Treatment Providers is dedicated to raising public awareness of addiction as a treatable disease and securing adequate reimbursement for treatment programs. This site is directed toward professional development and membership education. They offer the opportunity to apply for membership or request further information. Laypersons may not benefit significantly from this site.

BEHAVIORAL DISORDERS

ODD

`http://www.conductdisorders.com`

Try this Web site for more information on ODD and other conduct disorders.

National Center of PTSD (Post Traumatic Stress Disorder)

`http://www.ncptsd.org`

Available on this site are research and education on PTSD, training opportunities, and information for victims, trauma survivors, clinicians, researchers, and students.

The Something Fishy Web site on Eating Disorders

`http://www.something-fishy.org`

This site contains updates for information, Q & A, motivations for recovery, book recommendations, chatroom connections, and treatment options.

Cyberpsych Anxiety Disorders Page

`http://www.cyberpsych.org/anxdisor/anxiety.htm`

This meta-site has links to a variety of anxiety disorders including panic disorders, childhood phobias, and PTSD.

Anxiety Panic Internet Resources (tAPir)

`http://www.algy.com/anxiety`

Excellent resource for relaxation techniques, articles, diagnosis, prevention, links, and databases.

Bipolar Disorders Information Web Site

`http://www.mhsource.com/bipolar`

Online question and answer forum sponsored by Charles W. Bowden, M.D. and Alan Swann, M.D. the first Tuesday of each month from 10 to 11 P.M. (Eastern time). This site is operated by the Continuing Medical Education, Inc.

Dual Diagnosis Credentialed Listserv

`To subscribe email:Listserv@maelstrom.stjohns.edu`

The text of your message should read: subscribe DUALDIAG <your full name>

Dual Diagnosis Web Site

`http://www.erols.com/ksciacca`

Sciacca is comprehensive service development for mental illness, drug addiction and alcoholism (MIDAA). This site is designed to provide information and resources for service providers, consumers, and family members seeking assistance and education in this field.

Dual Diagnosis Online Dictionary of Mental Health

`http://www.human-nature.com/odmh/dual.html`

Sciacca hosts this Web site for co-occurring mental illness and substance disorders. Complete articles and chapters may be read and downloaded. Also included are a search engine and mailing lists.

For Today's Families (With Children and Adolescents With Brain Disorders)

`http://www.nami.org/youth/dualdigf.htm`

Fact page containing information on recovery for substance abuse and brain disorders (mental illness) as well as ADHD, depression, and bipolar disorder. Good information for families with adolescents.

PHYSICAL CONDITIONS

Teen Pregnancy Report

http://aspe.hhs.gov/hsp/teenp/97-98rpt.htm

Recently released online, this document, introduced in January, 1997, by the U.S. Department of Health and Human Services is the first annual report on the progress of the National Strategy to Prevent Teen Pregnancy. The report does contain some good news—teen birth rates have decreased nationally and in all states since 1991, falling twelve percent nationally and sixteen percent or more in seventeen states. The report contains statistics and analysis of teen birth and pregnancy rates, by age and race. It also details the strategies and partnerships forged by the HHS to continue this encouraging trend. Appendixes include Teenage Birth Rates in the United States, National and State Trends, 1990–96, an overview of various HHS teen pregnancy provision programs, and Teen Parent Provisions by State.

Teen Pregnancy

http://aspe.hhs.gov/hsp/teenp/intro.htm

The National Campaign to Prevent Teen Pregnancy has a very comprehensive site from parent brochures to resources they recommend. It may lead you in the direction of a curriculum. There are also awareness week materials for May.

American Foundation for AIDS Research

http://www.amfar.org/cgi-bin/iowa/index.html

The American Foundation for AIDS Research (AmFAR) is the nation's leading nonprofit organization dedicated to the support of AIDS research (both basic biomedical and clinical research), education for AIDS prevention, and sound AIDS-related public policy development.

Health On the Net Foundation

http://www.hon.ch

Health On the Net Foundation is a nonprofit organization whose mission is to build and support the international health and medical community on the Internet and World Wide Web, so that the potential benefits of this new communications medium may be realized by individuals, medical professionals, and healthcare providers. HON site includes a complete list of hospitals on the World Wide Web,

Internet medical support communities (listservers, newsgroups, and FAQs), medical sites, and search engines.

HIV InSite

`http://hivinsite.ucsf.edu`

HIV InSite is a project of the University of California, San Francisco, AIDS Program at San Francisco General Hospital, and the UCSF Center for AIDS Prevention Studies, which are programs of the UCSF AIDS Research Institute.

Medscape

`http://www.medscape.com`

This is a new, free Web site for health professionals and interested consumers. Practice-oriented information is peer-reviewed and edited by thought leaders in AIDS, infectious diseases, urology, and surgery. Highly-structured articles and full-color graphics are supplemental with stored literature searches and annotated links to relevant Internet resources. From SCP Communications, Inc., one of the world's leading publishers of medical journals and medical education programs.

VIOLENCE AND TRAUMA

The Beck Specialized Treatment Assessment Inventory for Adolescents (BSTAI-A) Research Edition

Email: `BeckAssociates@susquehanna-institute.com`
`http://www.susquehanna-institute.com`

This instrument has been used by counselors, psychologists, psychiatrists, juvenile justice, and family and children service professionals, as well as school professionals in various pilots. In a relatively non-threatening and open-ended manner, this protocol asks the questions in a way that allows the interview to access such things as the experiencing of, participating in, witnessing of, or being victimized by such things as physical violence or other forms of trauma.

Victims' Rights

`http://www.ojp.usdoj.gov/ovc/new/directions`

This recent report from the U.S. Department of Justice (USDOJ) Office for Victims of Crime (OVC) outlines a comprehensive plan for improving the rights of and services for crime victims in the United

States. While making some sixty-eight recommendations for improvement, the report also notes the advances that have been made in recent years, highlighting some of the hundreds of "innovative public policy initiatives and community partnerships that are revolutionizing the treatment of crime victims in America today." Users may download the full report in ASCII or .pdf format or view individual chapters in HTML, ASCII or .pdf formats.

CHILD ABUSE

The National Victim Center/Child Abuse Bibliography

http://www.ncjrs.org/txtfiles/163390.txt

Minnesota Center Against Violence and Abuse

http://www.mincava.umn.edu

SUICIDE/DEATH/DYING

Crisis, Grief and Healing: Men and Women

http://www.webhealing.com

PREVENTION SITES

Substance Abuse Treatment Facility Locator

http://findtreatment.samhsa.gov

This site offers a database providing a listing of federal, state, local, and private providers of alcoholism, drug abuse treatment, and prevention services by city, state, territory, and zip code.

Media Campaign in Action

http://www.mediacampaign.org/index.html

National youth anti-drug campaign.

Society for Prevention Research

http://www.oslc.org/spr/sprhome.html

The focus of this society is broadly defined and concerned with the problems pertaining to the prevention of drug and alcohol abuse and associated social maladjustment, crime, and behavior disorders.

PREVLINE: Prevention Online at the National Clearinghouse for Alcohol and Drug Information (NCADI)

http://www.samhsa.gov

PREVLINE is the name of the NCADI's multi-faceted online information activity. NCADI services include an information services staff equipped to respond to the public's alcohol, tobacco, and illicit drug (ATID) inquiries; the distribution of free ATID materials, including fact sheets, brochures, pamphlets, posters, and video tapes from an inventory of over 1,000 items; customized annotated bibliographies from alcohol and other drug databases consisting of over 36,000 records; a Prevention Materials Database (PMD); and Federal grant announcements and application kits for prevention programs, treatment, and research funding opportunities.

National Inhalant Prevention Coalition

http://www.inhalants.org

Synergies, a nonprofit corporation founded by Harvey J. Weiss and based in Austin, Texas, established the National Inhalant Prevention Coalition (NIPC) in 1992. The NIPC grew from a state-wide prevention project in Texas called the Texas Prevention Partnership which began in 1990. NIPC is a public–private effort to promote awareness and recognition of the problem of inhalant use. NIPC is funded in part by the Robert Wood Johnson Foundation and is led by Synergies.

American Academy of Addiction Psychiatry

http://www.aaap.org

The American Academy of Addiction Psychiatry was formed to promote excellence clinical practice in addiction psychiatry; educate the public to influence public policy regarding addictive illness; promote accessibility of quality treatment for all patients; provide continuing education for professionals in the field of addiction psychiatry; disseminate new information in the field of addiction psychiatry; and encourage research on the etiology, prevention, identification, and treatment of the addictions.

American Society of Addiction Medicine

http://www.asam.org

The nation's medical specialty society is dedicated to educating physicians and improving the treatment of individuals suffering from alcoholism or other addictions.

The Centers for Disease Control and Prevention's (CDC) National Prevention Information Network (NPIN)

http://www.cdcnpin.org

CDC's National Prevention Information Network is designed to facilitate sharing of HIV/AIDS, STD, and TB information and resources.

National Association of State Alcohol and Drug Abuse Directors (NASADAD)

http://www.nasadad.org/

This site links to conference announcements, community anti-drug coalitions and treatment innovations and initiations.

Safe and Drug Free Schools Program

http://www.ed.gov/offices/OESE/SDFS

TREATMENT STUDIES

Drug Abuse Treatment Outcome Study (DATOS)

http://www.datos.org

The Drug Abuse Treatment Outcome Study (DATOS) is NIDA's third national evaluation of treatment effectiveness. It is based on over 10,000 admissions during 1991–1993 to ninety-six community-based treatment programs in eleven large United States cities.

SUPPORT GROUPS

Eating Disorder Support Groups

http://www.hazelden.org

Overeaters Anonymous (OA) is based on the principles of AA.

Rational Recovery (RR) Support Group

http://rational.org/

RR was developed by Jack and Lois Trimpey. Jack has tended to focus on alcoholism and drug addiction. Lois has written mostly about food addictions. Evolved from RET.

Smart Recovery

http://www.smartrecovery.org/

This is a self management and recovery Web site featuring online recovery meetings Monday and Friday at 10:00 P.M. EST.

Clinical Psychology/Mental Health
MENTAL HEALTH SITES
BeckNet

http://www.susquehanna-institute.com

SEPI

http://www.cyberpsych.org/sepi

This site is run by the Society for the Exploration of Psychotherapy Integration

Albert Ellis Institute

http://www.rebt.org

Behavior Online

http://behavior.net

Radical Psychology Network

http://www.radpsynet.org

Association for the Advancement of Gestalt Therapy

http://www.aagt.org

Index of Health

http://www.chebucto.ns.ca/Health

Psychodrama

http://pages.nyu.edu/~as245/AITG

The Focusing Institute

http://www.focusing.org

Ecopsychology, Theory, and Practice

http://www.well.com/user/suscon/esalen/
ecopsyche.html

Art Therapy

http://www.arttherapy.org/

Self-Psychology Page

http://www.selfpsychology.org

Personality & Consciousness

http://pandc.ca/

Sketches of leading theorists.

Classic Theories of Child Development

http://childstudy.net/cdw.html

Narrative Psychology Internet and Resource Guide

http://web.lemoyne.edu/~hevern/narpsych.html

The Counselor Link

http://www.counselorlink.com

Psych Site

http://kenstange.com/psycsite

This Web site provides psychological resources.

Psych Web for Psychology Links

http://www.psychwww.com

Behavior OnLine: The Mental Health and Behavioral Science Meeting Place

http://www.behavior.net

Depression Central

http://www.psycom.net

National Depressive and Manic Depressive Association

http://www.ndmda.org

This site contains information and advocacy with links to support groups, patient/consumer reports, depression information, patient assistance programs, education, and diagnosis.

Internet Mental Health

http://www.mentalhealth.com

This site is an online resource for schizophrenia and other mental health information.

National Council for Community Behavioral Healthcare

http://www.nccbh.org

This site contains membership information, educational resources, a marketplace, a job bank, and public policy.

American Managed Behavioral Healthcare Association

http://www.ambha.org

These online resources contain membership, links to mental health sites, and reports and studies.

At Health Mental Health

http://www.athealth.com

This Web site contains a directory of professionals, newsletters, professional registration, treatment centers, a resource link, books for professionals and a psychotropic resource link.

NAMI

`http://www.nami.org`

National Alliance for the Mentally Ill produces this site, which contains the following links: book reviews, family support, a helpline, and legal issues for the mentally ill.

Kübler-Ross: Death and Dying

`http://www.elisabethkublerross.com`

MARRIAGE AND FAMILY SITES

KidsPsych

`http://www.kidspsych.org`

Developed by the American Psychological Association (APA), KidsPsych is a new "online adventure" for children and their parents. The Shockwave-powered site contains interactive games for children ages one through nine.

CURRENT TRENDS

Bazelon Center for Mental Health Law

`http://www.bazelon.org`

Based in Washington D.C., the Bazelon Center for Mental Health Law is a nonprofit legal advocacy organization for people with mental illness and mental retardation.

PsychNews Int'l

`Email: Psychnews@psychologie.de`
`Email: Pni@badlands.nodak.edu`

This site describes mental health related resources currently available, or announced, on the Internet. Submit all contributions or corrections for the Resource Update section to the PsychNews Int'l mailboxes.

Knowledge Exchange Network (KEN)

`http://www.mentalhealth.org`

KEN is a one-stop source of information and resources on prevention, treatment, and rehabilitation services for mental illness. KEN is a service of the Center for Mental Health Services, Substance

Abuse and Mental Health Services Administration, U.S. Department of Health and Human Services. KEN offers information related to Consumers/Survivors, Managed Care, Children's Mental Health, Statistics, and upcoming conferences and events. KEN offers an online database lookup of mental health resources around the country and in your community. KEN offers an extensive catalog of free publications, many of which can be viewed at the site or downloaded via FTP. All of the publications can be ordered via an online order form.

Childhood Sexual Abuse Manual

Email: sampson1@ix.netcom.com

The New York State Office of Mental Health is making available a manual to persons working with survivors of childhood sexual abuse. The manual is entitled *Understanding and Dealing with Sexual Abuse Trauma: An Educational Group for Women* and was written by Dr. Kristina Muenzenmaier, Donald Sampson, and others.

Sandplay Therapists of America

http://www.sandplayusa.org

Alzheimer Treatment and Cause

http://www.alz.org

Self Improvement Online

http://selfgrowth.com/therapy.html

This site contains sponsor Web sites and ninety-four additional related Web sites related to therapy and counseling.

JOURNALS

Psychwatch.com Counseling Journals

http://www.psychwatch.com/counsel_journals.htm

This meta-site links to forty counseling journals.

PSYCHOLOGY JOURNALS

American Psychiatric Association and American Psychological Association Online Journal

`http://www.journals.apa.org/prevention/`

A new online journal that is being jointly sponsored by the American Psychiatric Association and the American Psychological Association, by Martin E. P. Seligman and Donald F. Klein. It's also free and contains an email discussion list for subscribers to discuss the latest in psychological and psychiatric outcome/treatment research. Included is information on the Planetree model of patient-centered health care that is emerging as an alternative to traditional managed care. Interestingly, Planetree has not yet filtered down to mental health and counseling but is now represented by fifteen hospitals in the United States, as well as in Norway and England.

Psycoloquy

`http://psycprints.ecs.soton.ac.uk/`

Theory and Psychology Journal

`http://www.psych.ucalgary.ca/thpsyc/`

Pre- and Perinatal Psychology Journal

`http://www.birthpsychology.com/journal/index.html`

The Sport Psychologist

`http://www.humankinetics.com/`

Bulletin of the Menninger Clinic

`http://www.guilford.com/periodicals/jnme.htm`

Journal of Applied Psychology

`http://www.apa.org/journals/apl.html`

Journal of Social and Clinical Psychology

`http://www.guilford.com/periodicals/jnsc.htm`

Journal of Gerontology: Psychological Sciences

http://www.geron.org/journals/psychological.html

Journal of Humanistic Psychology

http://ahpweb.org/pub/journal/menu.html

Journal of Mind and Behavior

http://www.umaine.edu/jmb/

American Journal of Community Psychology

http://www.kluweronline.com/issn/0091-0562

APA Monitor

http://www.apa.org/monitor

Developmental Review

http://www.academicpress.com/dr

Journal of Divorce and Remarriage

http://www.haworthpressinc.com

Journal of Redecision Therapy

http://www.themetro.com/redecision

SOCIAL PSYCHOLOGY JOURNALS

American Journal of Sociology

http://www.journals.uchicago.edu/AJS/home.html

Social Psychology Quarterly

http://www.u.arizona.edu/~spq

Journal of Personality and Social Psychology

http://www.apa.org/journals/psp.html

Current Research in Social Psychology

http://www.uiowa.edu/~grpproc/crisp/crisp.html

Transactional Analysis Journal

http://www.tajnet.org

Social Cognition

http://www.guilford.com/periodicals/jnco.htm

Crisis (Journal of Crisis Intervention and Suicide Prevention)

http://www.hhpub.com/journals/crisis/index.html

Journal of Psychoeducational Assessment (JPA)

http://www.psychoeducational.com

Evidenced-Based Mental Health

http://www.ebmentalhealth.com

American Indian and Alaska Native Mental Health Research

http://www.uchsc.edu/ai/ncaianmhr/journal/index.htm

Internet Sites Useful in Social Work

The Social Work Mega-Sites

Association of Baccalaureate Social Work Program Directors

http://bpdonline.org/

This Web site, which serves as a home page for the BSW program directors, offers a variety of links to a wide range of social work Internet resources.

Columbia University Social Work Library

http://www.columbia.edu/cu/lweb/indiv/socwk/

Provides links to social work subject guides and Internet resources, social work related electronic journals on the Internet, and current social work monographs from Columbia University.

The Complete Social Worker Guide to Using the Internet in Social Work

http://www.geocities.com/Heartland/4862/cswhome.html

This online organization strives to create the most comprehensive knowledge base of social work professionals, educators, and students on the Web. They provide an impressive set of links to social work resources in a wide range of practice areas.

Computer Use in Social Services Network (CUSSN)

http://www2.uta.edu/cussn/

CUSSNet began in 1985 as a group of FIDONET bulletin boards. Possibly the first social work presence on the Internet, no set of links would be complete without including reference to this site. The site provides links to resources related to computer use in human services, and serves as an important linkage for social workers on the Internet.

Social Work Access Network

http://cosw.sc.edu/swan/

SWAN, sponsored by the University of South Carolina College of Social Work, offers one of the most complete listing of Internet resources available for social workers. SWAN organizes links in topical areas such as national organizations, global organizations, U.S. governments, schools of social work, conferences and meeting, and topics by subject. SWAN also has listserv and newsgroup directories.

Social Work and Social Services Web Sites

http://gwbweb.wustl.edu/library/websites.html

Hosted by the George Warren Brown School of Social Work, this site offers a tremendous number of links in a wide range of social work practice areas.

The Social Work Café

`http://www.geocities.com/Heartland/4862/swcafe.html`

This site represents a wealth of resources in a variety of areas for social workers. Hosted as a free service of GeoCities.Com, the Social Work Café is a community of global Social Work professionals, educators, and students who believe in the cross-global exchange of information.

Social Work Search.com

`http://www.socialworksearch.com/`

This site started in early 1996 as Tom Cleereman's Social Work Site. In April, 2001 Linkpopularity.com reported that over 900 different Web sites on the Internet provide links to socialworksearch.com. Now this former tiny personal Web site became a major portal for the online Social Work community in providing Internet related services to social workers and other helping professionals. Socialworksearch.com has now grown to more than 500 different web pages of services and Internet links, offering the largest online database of services devoted solely to the Social Work profession.

Information for Practice

`http://www.nyu.edu/socialwork/ip/`

The mission of Gary Holden's Information for Practice site is to help social service professionals throughout the world conveniently maintain an awareness of news regarding the profession and emerging scholarship. The goals of the project are to identify and deliver the highest quality information available in each category, regularly deliver and interesting mix of new information, create a more global sense of the profession for users from all locales, and to serve as a global socialization force for students.

Social Work Search .com

`http://www.socialworksearch.com/`

This site started in early 1996 as Tom Cleereman's Social Work Site. In April 2001, Linkpopularity.com reported that over 900 different Web sites on the Internet provide links to socialworksearch.com. Now this former tiny personal Web site became a major portal for the online Social Work community in providing Internet related services to social workers and other helping professionals. Socialworksearch.com has now grown to more than 500 different Web pages of services and

Internet links, offering the largest online database of services devoted solely to the Social Work profession.

Academic Sites

Grant MacEwan Community College (Alberta, Canada)

http://www.hcs.macewan.ca/socialwork/

Great list of aboriginal and international social work resources, with a focus on Canada.

Jane Addams College of Social Work (Illinois)

http://www.uic.edu/jaddams/college/

This site includes information about Hull House Museum, which commemorates the work of social welfare pioneer and peace advocate Jane Addams, her innovative settlement house associates, and the neighborhood they served.

Ohio State University

http://www.csw.ohio-state.edu/

This site features information about four journals sponsored by Ohio State College of Social Work, *Intervention, Journal of Poverty, Journal of Brief Therapy* and *Journal of Social Work Research and Evaluation.*

New Mexico State University

http://www.nmsu.edu/~socwork/

Provides information about the Family Preservation Institute and other social work related links.

State University of New York at Albany

http://www.albany.edu/ssw/

Offers information about the research activities of the School of Social Welfare.

Temple University (Pennsylvania)

http://www.temple.edu/socialwork/

Temple's Older Adult Protective Services Training Institute has been set up to provide educational opportunity and investigative consultation to the Commonwealth's 52 area agencies on aging and local law enforcement.

University of Bristol (UK)

http://www.bristol.ac.uk/sps/

The School for Policy Studies is the home of the Policy Press, and offers other social work links related to social policy in the United Kingdom.

University of Calgary (Alberta, Canada)

http://fsw.ucalgary.ca/

Easy-to-use site offers resources that are useful to students, faculty and staff at the Faculty of Social Work and others in the social work field. The University of Calgary offers *Currents: New Scholarship in the Human Services*, a scholarly, peer-reviewed journal developed with the goal of making quality academic publishing freely accessible.

University of Central Lancashire (UK)

http://www.uclan.ac.uk/facs/health/socwork/socihom1.htm

Provides access to useful links for social policy and social work.

University of Chicago (Illinois)

http://www.ssa.uchicago.edu/

This site offers the *Advocate's Forum,* a social work journal managed entirely by social work students.

University of East Anglia, Norwich (UK)

http://www.uea.ac.uk/menu/acad_depts/swk/

Provides information about the Centre for Research on the Child and Family and the Family Support Network.

University of Michigan

http://www.ssw.umich.edu/

Offers important resources for social work students and information about ongoing research at the University of Michigan.

University of Oxford (UK)

`http://marx.apsoc.ox.ac.uk/`

Provides information about current research at the University of Oxford, recent publications, and useful links.

University of Pennsylvania

`http://www.sp2.upenn.edu/`

The University of Pennsylvania site provides information about current research efforts of the School of Social Work.

University of Southern California

`http://www.usc.edu/dept/socialwork/`

USC offers the Rita and Maurice Hamovitch Social Work Research Center, which provides a wealth of links and resources for social work scholars.

University of Tennessee–Knoxville

`http://www.csw.utk.edu/`

Provides information about the Children's Mental Health Services Research Center, Veterinary Social Work Services and links to other important resources.

University of Texas at Austin

`http://www.utexas.edu/ssw/`

Provides a listing of the activities and publications of their Center for Social Work Research.

University of Utah

`http://www.socwk.utah.edu/`

The site provides information about ongoing research projects and related resources, including the Social Research Institute, the Belle S. Spafford Chair, and the Utah Justice Center.

University of Washington

`http://depts.washington.edu/sswweb/`

In addition to the usual links, UW offers *Policy Watch,* a more-or-less weekly bulletin about issues and events in Olympia during the legislative session, focused primarily on social welfare, low-income, and related health concerns before the legislature.

University of Wisconsin–Madison

http://socwork.wisc.edu/

Offers information about The Institute for Research on Poverty, The LaFollette Institute of Public Policy, and the UW Homelessness Project.

University of York (UK)

http://www.york.ac.uk/depts/spsw/

This UK site offers a useful Social Policy Resource Guide.

Washington University: George Warren Brown School of Social Work (Missouri)

http://gwbweb.wustl.edu/

One of the most comprehensive sites in social work education, these pages offer information about research projects at GWB and a complete list of informational links in a variety of practice areas. The Social Work and Social Services Jobs Database is a valuable resource for all social workers.

Government Resources

Administration for Children and Families

http://www.acf.dhhs.gov/

The Administration on Children, Youth and Families (ACYF) administers the major Federal programs that support: social services that promote the positive growth and development of children and youth and their families; protective services and shelter for children and youth in at-risk situations; child care for working families and families on public assistance; and adoption for children with special needs.

Bureau of the Census

http://www.census.gov/

The Census Bureau Web site is designed to enable intuitive use of their Internet offerings, so users need not to be familiar with the Census Bureau's internal organizational structure to effectively locate and use the resources the site has to offer.

Bureau of Justice Statistics

http://www.ojp.usdoj.gov/bjs/

BJS collects, analyzes, publishes, and disseminates information on crime, criminal offenders, victims of crime, and the operation of justice systems at all levels of government.

Bureau of Labor Statistics

http://stats.bls.gov/

The Bureau of Labor Statistics (BLS) is the principal fact-finding agency for the Federal Government in the broad field of labor economics and statistics. The BLS is an independent national statistical agency that collects, processes, analyzes, and disseminates essential statistical data to the American public, the U.S. Congress, other Federal agencies, State and local governments, business, and labor. The BLS also serves as a statistical resource to the Department of Labor.

Canadian Government Main Site

http://canada.gc.ca/

The Government of Canada Site is the Internet electronic access point through which Internet users around the world can obtain information about Canada, its government and its services. Direct links are also provided from this site to government departments and agencies that have Internet facilities.

Catalog of Federal Domestic Assistance

http://www.cfda.gov/

The Catalog of Federal Domestic Assistance Programs (CFDA) is a government-wide compendium of all 1,381 Federal programs, projects, services, and activities that provide assistance or benefits to the American public. These programs provide grants, loans, loan guarantees, services, information, scholarships, training, insurance, etc.

Centers for Disease Control

http://www.cdc.gov/

The Centers for Disease Control and Prevention (CDC), located in Atlanta, Georgia, USA, is an agency of the Department of Health and Human Services. Its mission is to promote health and quality of life by preventing and controlling disease, injury, and disability. The site provides health news, publications, software, data and statistics, and information about funding and programs.

Center for Substance Abuse Prevention

http://prevention.samhsa.gov/

CSAP's mission is to provide national leadership in the Federal effort to prevent alcohol, tobacco, and illicit drug problems. CSAP fosters the development of comprehensive, culturally appropriate prevention policies and systems that are based on scientifically defensible principles and target both individuals and the environments in which they live.

Center for Substance Abuse Treatment

http://csat.samhsa.gov/

The Center for Substance Abuse Treatment (CSAT) was created in October 1992 with the Congressional mandate to expand the availability of effective treatment and recovery services for alcohol and drug problems. CSAT works cooperatively across the private and public treatment spectrum to identify, develop, and support policies, approaches, and programs that enhance and expand treatment services for individuals who abuse alcohol and other drugs and that address individuals' addiction-related problems.

Centers for Medicare & Medicaid Services

http://www.cms.hhs.gov/

The Centers for Medicare and Medicaid Services (CMS), formerly the Health Care Financing Administration (HCFA), administers Medicare, Medicaid, related quality assurance programs, and other programs. It also makes certain that its beneficiaries are aware of the services for which they are eligible, that services are accessible, and that they are provided in an effective manner. CMS ensures that its policies and actions promote efficiency and quality within the total health care delivery system.

Child Support Enforcement

http://www.acf.dhhs.gov/programs/cse/

Child Support Enforcement helps States locate absent parents, establish paternity, and enforce legal orders for support.

Child Welfare Information Gateway

http://www.childwelfare.gov

Child Welfare Information Gateway promotes the safety, permanency, and well-being of children and families by connecting child welfare, adoption and related professionals as well as concerned citizens to timely, essential information. A service of the Children's Bureau, Administration for Children and Families, U.S. Department of Health and Human Services, the site provides access to print and electronic publications, websites, and online databases covering a wide range of topics from prevention to permanency, including child welfare, child abuse and neglect, adoption, search and reunion, and much more.

Corporation for National and Community Service

http://www.cns.gov/

This site provides information about volunteer opportunities, including VISTA, AmeriCorps, Senior Corps, Learn and Serve America, and National Service Scholarships.

Department of Health and Human Services (DHHS)

http://www.os.dhhs.gov/

The Department of Health and Human Services is the United States government's principal agency for protecting the health of all Americans and providing essential human services, especially for those who are least able to help themselves. It is the largest grant-making agency in the federal government, and it administers more grant dollars than all other federal agencies combined. HHS' Medicare program is the nation's largest health insurer, handling more than 1 billion claims per year.

Family and Youth Services Bureau

http://www.acf.hhs.gov/programs/fysb/

The mission of the Family and Youth Services Bureau (FYSB) is to provide national leadership on youth and family issues. The Bureau promotes positive outcomes for children, youth, and families by supporting a wide range of comprehensive services and collaborations at the local, Tribal, State, and national levels.

Federal Emergency Management Agency

http://www.fema.gov/

On March 1, 2003, the Federal Emergency Management Agency (FEMA) became part of the U.S. Department of Homeland Security (DHS). FEMA's continuing mission within the new department is to lead the effort to prepare the nation for all hazards and effectively manage federal response and recovery efforts following any national incident. FEMA also initiates proactive mitigation activities, trains first responders, and manages the National Flood Insurance Program.

FedWorld Information Network Home Page

http://www.fedworld.gov/

Access to thousands of U.S. Government Web sites, more than 500,000 U.S. government documents, databases, and other information products.

Government Printing Office

http://www.access.gpo.gov/

The Government Printing Office (GPO) prints, binds, and distributes the publications of the Congress as well as the executive departments and establishments of the Federal Government. Distribution is being accomplished on an increasing basis via various electronic media in accordance with Public Law 103-40, "The Government Printing Office Electronic Information Access Enhancement Act of 1993."

Healthfinder®

http://www.healthfinder.gov/

Healthfinder® is a gateway consumer health and human services information Web site from the United States government. Healthfinder® can lead you to selected online publications, clearinghouses, databases, Web sites, and support and self-help groups, as well as the government agencies and not-for-profit organizations that produce reliable information for the public. Launched in April 1997, Healthfinder® served Internet users over 1.7 million times in its first year online.

Health Resources and Services Administration

http://www.hrsa.gov/

The Health Resources and Services Administration (HRSA) directs national health programs which improve the health of the Nation by assuring quality health care to underserved, vulnerable and special-need populations and by promoting appropriate health professions workforce capacity and practice, particularly in primary care and public health.

House of Representatives

http://www.house.gov/

Contact your congressional representative the easy way.

Indian Health Service

http://www.ihs.gov/

The Indian Health Service (IHS), an agency within the Department of Health and Human Services, is responsible for providing federal health services to American Indians and Alaska Natives. The provision of health services to members of federally-recognized tribes grew out of the special government-to-government relationship between the federal government and Indian tribes.

Library of Congress

http://www.loc.gov/

The Library of Congress mission is to make its resources available and useful to the Congress and the American people and to sustain and preserve a universal collection of knowledge and creativity for future generations. This World Wide Web site allows the Library of Congress to historical collections, their catalog, the text and images from major exhibitions, the THOMAS database of current and historical information on the U.S. Congress, a Learning Page for K–12 students and teachers, and much more.

Maternal and Child Health Bureau

http://www.mchb.hrsa.gov/

The Maternal and Child Health Bureau (MCHB) is charged with the primary responsibility for promoting and improving the health of our Nation's mothers and children. It predecessor, the Children's Bureau, was established in 1912. In 1935, Congress enacted Title V of the Social Security Act, which authorized the Maternal and Child Health Services Programs—providing a foundation and structure for assuring the health of mothers and children now for more than 60 years. Today, Title V is administered by the Maternal and Child Health Bureau as part of the Health Resources and Services Administration, Public Health Service, U.S. Department of Health and Human Services.

National Cancer Institute

http://www.cancer.gov/

The National Cancer Institute (NCI) is a component of the National Institutes of Health (NIH), one of eight agencies that compose the Public Health Service (PHS) in the Department of Health and Human Services (DHHS). The NCI, established under the National Cancer Act of 1937, is the Federal Government's principal agency for cancer research and training. The National Cancer Act of 1971 broadened the scope and responsibilities of the NCI and created the National Cancer Program. Over the years, legislative amendments have maintained the NCI authorities and responsibilities and added new information dissemination mandates as well as a requirement to assess the incorporation of state-of-the-art cancer treatments into clinical practice.

The National Criminal Justice Reference Service

http://www.ncjrs.org/

The National Criminal Justice Reference Service (NCJRS) is one of the most extensive sources of information on criminal and juvenile justice in the world, providing services to an international community of policymakers and professionals. NCJRS is a collection of clearinghouses supporting all bureaus of the U.S. Department of Justice, Office of Justice Programs: the National Institute of Justice, the Office of Juvenile Justice and Delinquency Prevention, the Bureau of Justice Statistics, the Bureau of Justice Assistance, the Office for Victims of Crime, and the OJP Program Offices. It also supports the Office of National Drug Control Policy.

National Institute of Alcohol Abuse and Alcoholism

http://www.niaaa.nih.gov/

In 1970, the United States Congress recognized alcohol abuse and alcoholism as major public health problems and created the National Institute on Alcohol Abuse and Alcoholism (NIAAA) to combat them. The Web site provides information about reports and publications available from the Institute, as well as access to the ETOH database.

National Institute of Child Health and Human Development

http://www.nichd.nih.gov/

The National Institute of Child Health and Human Development is part of the National Institutes of Health, U.S. Department of Health and Human Services. The NICHD conducts and supports laboratory, clinical and epidemiological research on the reproductive, neurobiological, developmental, and behavioral processes that determine and maintain the health of children, adults, families and populations.

National Institute of Drug Abuse

http://www.nida.nih.gov/

The National Institute on Drug Abuse (NIDA) supports over 85 percent of the world's research on the health aspects of drug abuse and addiction, ranging from the most fundamental and essential questions about drug abuse; the molecule to managed care, and from DNA to community outreach research. The NIDA Web page is an important part of NIDA's effort to ensure the rapid and effective transfer of scientific data to policy makers, drug abuse practitioners, other health care practitioners and the general public.

National Institutes of Health

http://www.nih.gov/

The NIH mission is to uncover new knowledge that will lead to better health for everyone. NIH works toward that mission by: conducting research in its own laboratories; supporting the research of non-Federal scientists in universities, medical schools, hospitals, and research institutions throughout the country and abroad; helping in the training of research investigators; and fostering communication of biomedical information.

National Institute of Justice

http://www.ojp.usdoj.gov/nij/

The National Institute of Justice (NIJ) is the research agency of the U.S. Department of Justice. Created by the Omnibus Crime Control and Safe Streets Act of 1968, as amended, NIJ is authorized to support research, evaluation, and demonstration programs, development of technology, and both national and international information dissemination.

National Institute of Mental Health

http://www.nimh.nih.gov/

NIMH is the foremost mental health research organization in the world, with a mission of improving the treatment, diagnosis, and prevention of mental disorders such as schizophrenia and depressive illnesses, and other conditions that affect millions of Americans, including children and adolescents. The Web site provides information about mental health disorders, news and events, grants and contracts, and NIMH-sponsored research activities.

National Library of Medicine

http://www.nlm.nih.gov/

The NLM site provides individuals free access to MEDLINE for free. The visible human project and other offerings make this a "must browse" site.

National Institute on Aging

http://www.nia.nih.gov/

The National Institute on Aging (NIA) leads a broad scientific effort to understand the nature of aging and to extend the healthy, active years of life. In 1974, Congress granted authority to form the National Institute on Aging to provide leadership in aging research, training, health information dissemination, and other programs relevant to aging and older people. Subsequent amendments to this legislation designated the NIA as the primary federal agency on Alzheimer's disease research.

Office of Juvenile Justice and Delinquency Prevention

http://ojjdp.ncjrs.org/

The OJJDP Web site is designed to provide information and resources on both general areas of interest about juvenile justice and delinquency including conferences, funding opportunities, and new publications and the comprehensive strategy as a framework for communities to combat youth crime.

The Office of Minority Health

http://www.omhrc.gov/

The mission of the Office of Minority Health (OMH) is to improve and protect the health of racial and ethnic minority populations through the development of health policies and programs that will eliminate health disparities.

OMH was established in 1986 by the U.S. Department of Health and Human Services (HHS). It advises the Secretary and the Office of Public Health and Science on public health program activities affecting American Indians and Alaska Natives, Asian Americans, Blacks/

African Americans, Hispanics/Latinos, Native Hawaiians, and other Pacific Islanders.

Office of Population Affairs

http://opa.osophs.dhhs.gov

The Office of Population Affairs provides resources and policy advice on population, family planning, reproductive health, and adolescent pregnancy issues. OPA also administers two grant programs, the national Family Planning Program and the Adolescent Family Life Program.

PREVLINE: Prevention Online

http://www.health.org/

The National Clearinghouse for Alcohol and Drug Information, NCADI, is the world's largest repository of information on substance abuse prevention and policy. PREVLINE presents information on drug and alcohol abuse, alcoholism prevention, overdoses, addiction, and treatment through links to thousands of documents, searchable databases, statistics, press releases, public domain graphics, and interactive forums.

Rural Empowerment Zones and Enterprise Community Program

http://www.ezec.gov/

The Rural Empowerment Zone/Enterprise Community Program Home Page is designed to promote the exchange of information about the Presidential Empowerment Initiative. Here you will find information about the purposes and organization of the Initiative and the Empowerment Zones, Enterprise Communities, and Champion Communities participating in the Initiative. In addition, the REZ/EC Home Page provides a toolbox of information to help communities develop and implement effective strategic plans for community and economic development.

Rural Housing Service

http://www.rurdev.usda.gov/rhs/

The USDA Rural Housing Service has various programs available to aid in the development of rural America. Rural Housing programs are divided into three categories: Community Facilities (CF), Single Family Housing (SFH), and Multi-Family Housing (MFH). These programs were formerly operated by the Rural Development Administration and the Farmers Home Administration.

Senate Home Page

http://www.senate.gov/

Contact your Senators the easy way.

Social Security Administration

http://www.ssa.gov/

Social Security Online provides a wealth of information about the Social Security Administration, enabling users to better negotiate the maze of services available.

Substance Abuse and Mental Health Services Administration

http://www.samhsa.gov/

SAMHSA's mission is to assure that quality substance abuse and mental health services are available to the people who need them and to ensure that prevention and treatment knowledge is used more effectively in the general health care system.

Thomas—U.S. Congress on the Internet

http://thomas.loc.gov/

Current U.S. Federal Legislative Information, including bills, laws, Congressional Record, reports, and links to further information.

Veterans Affairs

http://www.va.gov/

The Department of Veterans Affairs (VA) Web site provides information on VA programs, veteran's benefits, VA facilities worldwide, and VA medical automation software. The site serves several major constituencies including the veteran and his/her dependents, Veterans Service Organizations, the military, the general public, and VA employees around the world. Documents on the site are linked from their table of contents and searchable by keyword.

White House

http://www.whitehouse.gov/

This site links users to the executive branch of the United States government. The site includes an archive of White House documents.

Professional Association Sites

American Association of Community Psychiatrists

http://www.comm.psych.pitt.edu/

The AACP seeks to promote and maintain excellence in the care of patients through the organization of psychiatrists practicing community mental health on state, regional and national levels.

American Association for Marriage and Family Therapy

http://www.aamft.org/

The American Association for Marriage and Family Therapy (AAMFT) is the professional association for the field of marriage and family therapy. We represent the professional interests of more than 23,000 marriage and family therapists throughout the United States, Canada and abroad.

American Association of Pastoral Counselors

http://www.aapc.org/

Pastoral Counseling is a mental health discipline that integrates psychotherapy and spirituality. Pastoral Counselors are mental health professionals who have received specialized graduate training in both religion and the behavioral sciences, and practice the integrated discipline of pastoral counseling. The American Association of Pastoral Counselors (AAPC) represents and sets professional standards for over 3,200 Pastoral Counselors and more than 100 pastoral counseling centers in the United States.

American Association of Health Plans

http://www.aahp.org/

The American Association of Health Plans (AAHP), located in Washington, DC, represents more than 1,000 HMOs, PPOs and other network-based plans. The site offers a wealth of information related to health care and legislative advocacy.

American Counseling Association

http://www.counseling.org/

The American Counseling Association is a not-for-profit, professional and educational organization that is dedicated to the growth and enhancement of the counseling profession.

American Medical Association

http://www.ama-assn.org/

Since its founding in 1847 by a group of physicians concerned about advancing the quality of medical education, science, and practice, the American Medical Association's core purpose has been to promote the art and science of medicine and the betterment of public health.

American Mental Health Counselors Association

http://www.amhca.org/

The mission of the American Mental Health Counselors Association is to enhance the profession of mental health counseling through licensing, advocacy, education, and professional development. Their vision is to be the national organization representing licensed mental health counselors, and state chapters, with consistent standards of education, training, licensing, practice, advocacy, and ethics.

American Psychiatric Association

http://www.psych.org/

The American Psychiatric Association is a medical specialty society recognized worldwide. Its 40,500 U.S. and international physicians specialize in the diagnosis and treatment of mental and emotional illnesses and substance use disorders.

American Public Health Association

http://www.apha.org/

The American Public Health Association (APHA) is the oldest and largest organization of public health professionals in the world, representing more than 50,000 members from over 50 occupations of public health.

Association for Behavior Analysis

http://www.abainternational.org/

The Association for Behavior Analysis is dedicated to promoting the experimental, theoretical, and applied analysis of behavior. It encompasses contemporary scientific and social issues, theoretical advances, and the dissemination of professional and public information.

Association for Community Organization and Social Administration

http://www.acosa.org/

The Association for Community Organization and Social Administration, formed in 1987, is a membership organization for community organizers, planners, activists, administrators, policy practice specialists, students, and professors. ACOSA members represent a variety of disciplines and professional fields that strive to strengthen community organization and social administration in social work practice and education.

Association for Oncology Social Work

http://www.aosw.org/

A nonprofit, international organization dedicated to the enhancement of psychosocial services to people with cancer and their families. AOSW is dedicated to increasing awareness about the social, emotional, educational, and spiritual needs of cancer patients. It supports its members' commitment to helping and advocating for cancer patients by providing continuing education through conferences and publications; promoting clinical research; and fostering networking to address common issues and concerns.

Association of Baccalaureate Program Directors

http://bpdonline.org/

This professional association represents directors of baccalaureate social work programs accredited through the Council on Social Work Education.

Association of Social Work Boards

http://www.aswb.org/

The Association of Social Work Boards (ASWB) is the association of boards that regulate social work. Incorporated in 1979 as the American Association of State Social Work Boards, an organization devoted to consumer protection, ASWB membership now includes 49 states, the District of Columbia, the Virgin Islands, and Alberta, Canada.

Australian Association of Social Work

http://www.aasw.asn.au/

The objectives of the Australian Association of Social Workers Ltd. are to promote the profession of social work, to provide an organization through which social workers can develop a professional identity, to establish, monitor and improve practice standards, to contribute to the development of social work knowledge, to advocate on behalf of clients, and to actively support social structures and policies pursuant to the promotion of social justice.

British Association of Social Workers

http://www.basw.co.uk/

BASW is the largest organization of professional social workers in the United Kingdom. They speak on all issues that affect the professional standing of social work. Members come from a wide range of agencies in the Local Authority, Voluntary, Independent and Private sectors throughout the United Kingdom. BASW campaigns for improvements to legislation, for social justice and the quality of social work services and good practice.

Clinical Social Work Federation

http://www.cswf.org/

The Clinical Social Work Federation is a confederation of 31 state societies for clinical social work. Their state societies are formed as voluntary associations for the purpose of promoting the highest standards of professional education and clinical practice. Each society is active with legislative advocacy and lobbying efforts for adequate and appropriate mental health services and coverage at their state and national levels of government.

Computer Use in Social Services Network

http://www2.uta.edu/cussn/

The Computer Use in Social Services Network (CUSSN) is an informal association of professionals interested in exchanging information and experiences on using computers in the human services. It has been in existence since 1981.

Council on Social Work Education

http://www.cswe.org/

CSWE is a national association that preserves and enhances the quality of social work education for practice that promotes the goals of individual and community well being and social justice. CSWE pursues this mission through setting and maintaining policy and program standards, accrediting bachelor's and master's degree programs in social work, promoting research and faculty development, and advocating for social work education.

HUSITA: Human Service Information Technology Applications

http://www.husita.org/

Husita is an international association of information technology (IT) innovators in human services dedicated to promoting the ethical and effective use of IT to better serve humanity. Husita's focus and expertise is situated at the intersection of three core domains: information technology; human services and social development. With an emphasis on human centeredness and social justice, Husita strives to promote international knowledge development, dissemination and transfer of technology within human services. It achieves this through multidisciplinary leadership in international conferences, publications, collaboration and consultation directed particularly at IT applications and innovations that promote social betterment.

Institute for Mental Health Initiatives

http://www.gwumc.edu/sphhs/imhi/

Institute for Mental Health Initiatives (IMHI), a nonprofit organization of mental health professionals, promotes emotional well being in children, families, and their communities. It makes mental health research accessible to the media and the general public. IMHI builds bridges between clinicians and researchers in the field of mental health, the general public, and the members of the media.

International Association of Group Psychotherapy

http://www.iagp.com/

The purpose of the IAGP is to serve the development of group psychotherapy, as a field of practice, training, and scientific study, by means of international conferences, publications, and other forms of communication. The assumption is that there is mutual respect between representatives of differing theories and practices concerned with the use and study of group resources in psychotherapy and in dealing with other human problems.

International Federation of Social Workers

http://www.ifsw.org/

The International Federation of Social Workers is a successor to the International Permanent Secretariat of Social Workers, which was founded in Paris in 1928 and was active until the outbreak of World War II. It was not until 1950, at the time of the International Conference of Social Work in Paris, that the decision was made to create the International Federation of Social Workers, an international organization of professional social workers.

Irish Association of Social Workers

http://www.iasw.ie/

The Irish Association of Social Workers (IASW) was founded in 1971. It is the national organization of professional social workers in the Republic of Ireland.

Latino Social Workers Organization

http://www.lswo.org/

The Latino Social Workers Organization provides information resources and networking for Latino social workers and social work students.

Mental Health in Corrections Consortium

http://www.forest.edu/mhcca/

MHCC is dedicated to being a leading voice for mental health providers within the criminal justice system, primarily corrections, and providing the highest quality of training related to mental health issues within criminal justice.

National Alliance for Hispanic Health

http://www.hispanichealth.org/

The National Alliance for Hispanic Health focuses on the health, mental health, and human services needs of the diverse Hispanic communities. The Alliance's membership consists of thousands of front-line health and human services providers and organizations serving Hispanic communities. The organization was founded in Los Angeles in 1973 as the Coalition of Spanish-Speaking Mental Health Organizations to represent and advocate for the mental health needs of Mexican American, Puerto Rican, Cuban American, Central American, and South American communities in the United States.

The National Association of Black Social Workers (NABSW)

http://www.nabsw.org/

The National Association of Black Social Workers, Inc. is designed to promote the welfare, survival, and liberation of communities of African ancestry. Members of the NABSW recognize the necessity of Black community control and accountability of self to the Black community.

National Association of Social Workers (NASW)

http://www.socialworkers.org/

NASW is the largest association of professional social workers in the United States. With more than 155,000 members in 56 chapters, NASW promotes, develops and protects the practice of social work and social workers. NASW also seeks to enhance the well being of individuals, families, and communities through its work and through its advocacy.

National Association of State Mental Health Program Directors

http://www.nasmhpd.org/

The National Association of State Mental Health Program Directors (NASMHPD) organizes to reflect and advocate for the collective interests of State Mental Health Authorities and their directors at the national level. NASMHPD analyzes trends in the delivery and financing of mental health services and builds and disseminates knowledge and experience reflecting the integration of public mental health programming in evolving healthcare environments.

National Council for Community Behavioral Healthcare

http://www.nccbh.org/

The National Council for Community Behavioral Healthcare was founded in 1970 to implement a vision and set of beliefs through membership, advocacy and education. Through their work in the public interest, they advocate before the White House, Congress, and federal agencies to advance the interests of our members and the consumers that they serve.

Society for Social Work and Research

http://www.sswr.org/

The Society for Social Work and Research was founded in 1994 as a freestanding organization that works collaboratively with other organizations that are committed to improving the support for research among social workers.

Society for Social Work Leadership in Healthcare

`http://www.sswlhc.org/`

The Society for Social Work Leadership in Healthcare is an association dedicated to promoting the universal availability, accessibility, coordination, and effectiveness of health care that addresses the psychosocial components of health and illness.

World Federation of Mental Health

`http://www.wfmh.com/`

The World Federation for Mental Health is an international nonprofit advocacy organization founded in 1948 to advance, among all peoples and nations, the prevention of mental and emotional disorders, the proper treatment and care of those with such disorders, and the promotion of mental health. The Federation achieves its goals through public education programs such as World Mental Health Day, research through collaborating centers at major universities, consultation to the United Nations and its specialized agencies, and a regional structure for organizing project work at the community level.

Electronic Journals and Newsletters

Action Research International

`http://www.scu.edu.au/schools/gcm/ar/ari/arihome.html`

Action Research International is a refereed on-line journal of action research. Published in Australia, it has an international editorial panel and is sponsored by the Institute of Workplace Research Learning and Development within the Graduate College of Management at Southern Cross University.

The Advocate's Forum

`http://www.ssa.uchicago.edu/publications/advoforum.shtml`

A social work journal managed entirely by University of Chicago students with support from the Office of External Affairs. Inside you will find substantive articles reflecting the diversity of interests, ideas, and concerns of social work students and graduates.

Age and Ageing

http://ageing.oxfordjournals.org/

An international journal publishing refereed original articles and commissioned reviews on geriatric medicine and gerontology. Its range includes research on aging and clinical, epidemiological, and psychological aspects of later life.

AIDS Book Review Journal

http://www.uic.edu/depts/lib/aidsbkrv

An electronic journal reviewing books, videos, journal titles, and other materials covering AIDS, safer sex, sexually transmitted diseases, and other related materials, published irregularly by the University of Illinois at Chicago Library.

Alcohol Alerts

http://www.niaaa.nih.gov/Publications/
AlcoholAlerts/

A quarterly bulletin of the National Institute on Alcohol Abuse and Alcoholism that disseminates important research findings on a single aspect of alcohol abuse and alcoholism.

American Journal on Addictions

http://www.aaap.org/journal/journalindex.htm

Contents of issues and abstracts of articles from *AJA,* an authoritative source of new information on drug abuse and the addictions.

American Medical Association Publishing

http://pubs.ama-assn.org/

Web editions of the AMA's Scientific Publications and *American Medical News* and links to condition-specific Web sites.

APA Addictions Newsletter

http://www.kumc.edu/addictions_newsletter/

An online publication of The American Psychological Association, Division 50.

APA Journals

http://www.apa.org/journals/

A listing of all journals published by the American Psychological Association.

Canadian Journal of Behavioural Science

http://www.cpa.ca/cjbs.htm

Abstracts and full-text versions of articles.

The CATO Journal

http://www.cato.org/pubs/journal/index.html

Founded in 1977, the Cato Institute is a nonpartisan public policy research foundation headquartered in Washington, D.C. The Cato Institute seeks to broaden the parameters of public policy debate to allow consideration of more options that are consistent with the traditional American principles of limited government, individual liberty, and peace. *The Cato Journal* is an interdisciplinary journal of public policy analysis.

Child and Adolescent Psychiatry

http://www.priory.co.uk/psychild.htm

Online journal featuring articles relevant to the treatment of children and adolescents.

Child Maltreatment

http://www.sagepub.com/journal.aspx?pid=15

Child Maltreatment is the main vehicle of the American Professional Society on the Abuse of Children. Its purpose is to publish longer and more in-depth analyses of theoretical, practice, and policy issues. In addition, CM is an outlet for high-quality original empirical research and reviews of the research literature. It is now available electronically.

Child Welfare Review

http://www.childwelfare.com/kids/news.htm

An electronic journal for coverage of issues related to the well being of children. It contains both links to articles related to child welfare and original articles.

The Chronicle of Philanthropy

`http://philanthropy.com/`

The Chronicle of Philanthropy is an important news source for charity leaders, fund raisers, grant makers, and other people involved in philanthropic enterprise.

Current Research in Social Psychology

`http://www.uiowa.edu/~grpproc/crisp/crisp.html`

A peer reviewed, electronic journal covering all aspects of social psychology sponsored by the Center for the Study of Group Processes at the University of Iowa.

Electronic Journals and Periodicals in Psychology and Related Fields

`http://psych.hanover.edu/Krantz/journal.html`

A regularly updated listing of psychology-relevant journals.

The Future of Children

`http://www.futureofchildren.org/`

Produced by the Center for the Future of Children, The David and Lucile Packard Foundation, *The Future of Children* is published three times a year and (mostly) reproduced on this site. Links to previous editions are available.

Harvard Mental Health Letter

`http://www.health.harvard.edu/newsletters/`
`Harvard_Mental_Health_Letter.htm`

Selected articles from the paper publication.

Hunger Notes

`http://www.worldhunger.org/`

Hunger Notes is an online journal that is sponsored by the World Hunger Education Service.

Journal of Applied Behavior Analysis

`http://seab.envmed.rochester.edu/jaba/`

Abstracts and tables of contents.

Journal of Children and Poverty

http://www.tandf.co.uk/journals/carfax/10796126.html

The Journal of Children and Poverty is a publication of the Institute for Children and Poverty, the research and training division of Homes for the Homeless. It offers a forum for the presentation of research and policy initiatives in the areas of education, social services, public policy, and welfare reform as they affect children, youth, and families in poverty.

Journal of Cognitive Rehabilitation

http://www.jofcr.com

A specialized online magazine containing general interest articles, personal experience articles, research reports and computerized therapy exercises related to brain injury, head injury, and strokes.

Journal of Mind and Behavior

http://www.umaine.edu/jmb/

Journal related to cross-causal understanding of cognition and behavior. Contents and abstracts of articles in past issues.

The Journal of Online Behavior (JOB)

http://www.behavior.net/JOB/

JOB is concerned with the empirical study of human behavior in the online environment, and with the impact of evolving communication and information technology upon individuals, groups, organizations, and society. It is a peer-reviewed, behavioral science/social science journal, with editorial board members from several countries and disciplinary affiliations. The journal is published electronically on the World Wide Web, and in printed form. Each article published on the Web is accompanied by an interactive discussion space, a pointer to which will accompany the article site. Significant comments from discussions may accompany the paper publication.

Journal of Poverty

http://www.journalofpoverty.org/

The Journal of Poverty: Innovations on Social, Political and Economic Inequalities is the first refereed journal designed to provide a focused outlet for discourse on poverty and inequality.

Journal of Social Work Practice

http://www.tandf.co.uk/journals/carfax/02650533.html

The Journal of Social Work Practice publishes refereed articles devoted to the exploration and practice of social welfare and allied health professions from psychodynamic and systemic perspectives.

The New Social Worker Online

http://www.socialworker.com/

The New Social Worker is the only national magazine devoted to social work students and recent graduates. This Web site presents the online version of the magazine, and presents links to employment resources.

NIH Record

http://www.nih.gov/nihrecord/

The NIH Record is the biweekly newsletter for employees of the National Institutes of Health.

Nursing Center

http://www.nursingcenter.com/

The American Journal of Nursing was the first U.S. nursing publication to make a home on the World Wide Web. It has recently launched NursingCenter, which features full-text continuing education articles as well as tables of contents from the current *AJN*, summaries of articles, and links to sites for other nursing journals.

PSYCLINE: Your Guide to Psychology and Social Science Journals on the Web

http://www.psycline.org/journals/psycline.html

A directory of links to more than 1,800 psychology and social science journal sites, this Web site covers English, French, and Dutch language journals, and provides general journal information, tables of contents, abstracts, or full text articles.

On the Issues: The Progressive Woman's Quarterly

http://www.ontheissuesmagazine.com/

This Internet-only journal presents articles on international and domestic affairs, political analysis, philosophy, religion and spirituality, health and medicine, arts, culture, social and personal issues.

Philanthropy News Digest

`http://fdncenter.org/pnd/`

The Foundation Center publishes electronically its *Philanthropy News Digest* every week, highlighting philanthropy-related news from other print and electronic periodicals nationwide.

Proceedings of the National Academy of Sciences

`http://www.pnas.org/`

PNAS is one of the world's most-cited multidisciplinary scientific serials. Since its establishment in 1915, it continues to publish cutting-edge research reports, commentaries, reviews, perspectives, colloquium papers, and actions of the Academy. Coverage in PNAS spans the biological, physical, and social sciences. PNAS is published biweekly in print, and weekly online in PNAS Early Edition.

Psychiatric Times

`http://www.psychiatrictimes.com/`

Full text of news and clinical articles for psychiatrists, allied mental health professionals and primary care physicians who treat mental disorders.

Psychiatry on Line

`http://www.priory.co.uk/psycont.htm`

Current contents and more from the *International Journal of Psychiatry*.

Psychotherapy Finances

`http://www.psyfin.com`

A newsletter related to topics private practitioners need to know about: practice building; marketing tips; hot niche market opportunities; health reform initiatives; plus managed care news and even tax tips.

PSYCHE

http://psyche.cs.monash.edu.au/

A refereed electronic journal dedicated to supporting the interdisciplinary exploration of the nature of consciousness and its relation to the brain.

Psychological Science Agenda

http://www.apa.org/science/psa/

The newsletter of the American Psychological Association Science Directorate.

Psycoloquy

http://psycprints.ecs.soton.ac.uk/

A refereed international, interdisciplinary electronic journal sponsored by the American Psychological Association (APA), publishing target articles and peer commentary in all areas of psychology as well as cognitive science, neuroscience, behavioral biology, artificial intelligence, robotics/vision, linguistics and philosophy.

Qualitative Report

http://www.nova.edu/ssss/QR/

An online journal dedicated to qualitative research and critical inquiry.

Social Policy

http://www.socialpolicy.org/

Electronic magazine about social and political movements and issues. Provides articles, a message board, and links to related resources.

Social Research Update

http://www.soc.surrey.ac.uk/sru/

A quarterly publication by the Department of Sociology, University of Surrey, England. Each issue covers one topic in sufficient depth to indicate the main directions of recent developments and provide a bibliography for further reading.

Social Service Review

http://www.journals.uchicago.edu/SSR/

Contents, author notes, and full-text articles from one of the premier journals in social work.

Sociological Research Online

http://www.socresonline.org.uk/

Online journal that publishes peer reviewed articles applying sociological analysis to a wide range of topics.

Standards: An International Journal of Multicultural Studies

http://www.colorado.edu/journals/standards/

An online publication featuring art, fiction, and scholarly essays relating to multicultural studies.

Technology in Human Services

http://www2.uta.edu/cussn/jths/

Technology in Human Services is a journal dedicated to providing information about the use of computer-based information technologies in the human services. It is designed for practitioners as well as educators.

Social Work Areas of Practice Sites

ADMINISTRATION

Action Without Borders

http://www.idealist.org/

Organization with an aim to create a global network of community-based centers that will link, serve, and strengthen individuals and organizations working to build a better world.

Aspen Institute

http://www.aspeninstitute.org/

This site offers information on the activities and programs of the Aspen Institute in the U.S. and in Germany, France, Italy and Japan. The Aspen Institute is dedicated to the development of leadership in the nonprofit sector.

BoardSource

http://www.boardsource.org/

BoardSource, formerly the National Center for Nonprofit Boards, was established in 1988 by the Association of Governing Boards of Universities and Colleges (AGB) and INDEPENDENT SECTOR. The Web site provides information on BoardSource's activities, including its training, education, and consulting services for nonprofit boards. The site also features a catalog of materials on nonprofit governance published by BoardSource, and also includes a Knowledge Center which provides answers and information on nonprofit governance.

Council on Foundations

http://www.cof.org/

Features information on the Council, which is dedicated to assisting grantmakers become more effective fundraisers and to supporting the growth of organized philanthropy.

Foundation Center

http://fdncenter.org/

A nonprofit information clearinghouse, providing information on foundations and corporate giving. The Center's site includes information on the Center, its libraries, seminars and publications. The site also features grantmaker information (including links to grantmaker Web sites), a searchable database of philanthropy-related articles, and a section on the fundraising process, including a proposal writing short course.

Free Management Library

http://www.managementhelp.org/

The Free Management Library (formerly the Nonprofit Managers' Library) facilitates sharing of free, online, and how-to management resources among nonprofits—including fundraising and grant writing, marketing and public relations, using the Internet, and evaluation. The Management Assistance Program (MAP) for Nonprofits in St. Paul, Minnesota administers the library.

GuideStar

http://www.guidestar.org/

Information on the programs and finances of more than 700,000 American nonprofits organizations, with up-to-date news stories and features on philanthropy, and a forum for donors and volunteers.

Independent Sector

http://www.independentsector.org/

Presents the various aspects of Independent Sector, a national coalition of voluntary organizations, foundations, and corporate giving programs, including information on Independent Sector's advocacy, research, and leadership programs.

Introducing New Technology Successfully into an Agency

http://www.coyotecom.com/tech/techbuy.html

Introducing computers to your agency, or upgrading software or hardware your agency uses, will change the way you access and manage information—for the better, you hope. But without realistic expectations and a thoughtful strategy, a new system can create as many problems as it is supposed to solve. This tip sheet can help.

The Joseph and Matthew Payton Philanthropic Studies Library

http://www-lib.iupui.edu/special/ppsl.html

The mission of the philanthropic studies collection is to support the educational and research programs of the Indiana University Center on Philanthropy.

The Management Assistance Program for Nonprofits

http://mapnp.nonprofitoffice.com/

MAP for Nonprofits primarily works with nonprofit organizations in the Greater Twin Cities Metropolitan Area of Minneapolis and St. Paul. Their Web site contains information about services they provide to nonprofits and a library of information helpful to social work administrators.

Nonprofit Cyber-Accountability

http://www.charitychannel.com/forums/cyb-acc/resources/

Offers the Cyber-Accountability listserv, an ongoing discussion on the nonprofit world and the use of information technology. The site also provides information on the National Accountability Research

Project at the Nonprofit Coordinating Committee of New York, as well as links to other sites that contain information on nonprofits.

OpportunityKnocks

`http://www.opportunitynocs.org/`

A resource for nonprofit jobs and employment opportunities. Job seekers can conduct free searches through our large database of available nonprofit jobs online, while nonprofit organizations can post help wanted classified ads for job openings online.

Philanthropy News Network Online

`http://pnnonline.org/`

The Web site has extensive resources with alerts and links to many nonprofit sites, including a Meta-Index comprehensive text list of resources on the Internet of interest to nonprofits.

PRAXIS

`http://www.sp2.upenn.edu/~restes/praxis.html`

Resources for social and economic development; pointers to many resources created by Dr. Richard J. Estes at the University of Pennsylvania.

Strategic Communications Toolkit

`http://www.benton.org/publibrary/toolkits/stratcommtool.html`

This is a list of Internet and other resources aimed at helping nonprofits make better use of information and communications technologies in their work.

Strategic Planning (in nonprofit or for-profit organizations)

`http://www.mapnp.org/library/plan_dec/str_plan/str_plan.htm`

Sponsored by The Management Assistance Program for Nonprofits in Minneapolis, this site provides an overview of a variety of perspectives about strategic planning and a variety of approaches used in the strategic planning. The site also includes guidelines for the reader to carry out planning according to the nature and needs of their organization. The MAP provides technology grants to nonprofit organizations, and the site includes a useful section on technology planning.

TechFoundation—Technology for Nonprofits

http://techfoundation.org/

TechFoundation is a Cambridge-based, nonprofit organization that delivers technology, expertise and capital to help nonprofit organizations serve humanity. TechFoundation envisions a world where nonprofit organizations can access the same resources to serve humanity that businesses use to create wealth.

TechSoup.Org: The Technology Place for Nonprofits

http://techsoup.org/

TechSoup is a trusted technology resource that offers a variety of information and services for the benefit of the nonprofit sector. TechSoup provides instructional articles and worksheets for nonprofit staff members who utilize information technologies, as well as technology planning information for executives and other decision makers. Their introductory articles and message board support are aimed at those who do not have much experience using technology, but the site also provides more advanced information.

Urban Institute

http://www.urban.org/

Provides information on the activities of the Institute and its research and policy centers, and programs. The site also presents briefings on topical issues.

Volunteer Match

http://www.volunteermatch.org/

VolunteerMatch is a leader in the nonprofit world dedicated to helping everyone find a great place to volunteer. The organization offers a variety of online services to support a community of nonprofit, volunteer and business leaders committed to civic engagement. This popular service welcomes millions of visitors a year and has become the preferred internet recruiting tool for more than 40,000 nonprofit organizations.

AGING

Administration on Aging

http://www.aoa.dhhs.gov/

Information about the Administration on Aging and its programs for the elderly, information about resources for practitioners who serve the aged, statistical information on the aging, and information for consumers (older persons and their families) including how to obtain services for senior citizens and electronic booklets on aging related issues. It also includes a link to AoA's National Aging Information Center and extensive links to other aging related Web resources.

Alzheimer's Association

http://www.alz.org/

The home page of the Alzheimer's association in the United States. Contains information about chapters, caregiver resources, medical information, public policy, and links to other resources.

Alzheimer's Disease Resource Page

http://www.ohioalzcenter.org/resource.html

Hosted by Case Western Reserve University, this page provides information on Alzheimer's disease, for caregivers, practitioners, researchers, and the general public.

ALZwell Caregiver Support

http://www.alzwell.com/

ALZwell Caregiver Support is dedicated to helping dementia caregivers to find understanding, wisdom and support throughout the caregiving journey.

APA Division 20

http://apadiv20.phhp.ufl.edu/

The home page of Division 20 of the American Psychological Association (Adult Development and Aging). This site provides information about the mission of Division 20, research and employment opportunities, pre- and post-doctoral programs of study in adult development and aging, instructional resources for teachers of adult development and aging, directory of members, contact information for specific laboratories/centers and institutes, and a Resource Guide for Clinicians.

Association for Gerontology Education in Social Work: AGE-SW

http://www.agesocialwork.org/

Provides information about the organization, gerontology-related resources, and highlights from *AGEnda,* the AGE-SW newsletter.

ElderCare Online

http://www.ec-online.net/

ElderCare Online is for people caring for aging loved ones. They are committed to providing an online community where supportive peers and professionals help improve quality of life for caregivers and their elder. Includes newsletter, discussion forums, and helpful information.

Family Caregiver Alliance

http://www.caregiver.org/

Information about the Family Caregiver Alliance, resource centers in California, caregiver tips, statistics and research, public policy, information about educational programs and conferences, publications, and more.

Geropsychology Central

http://www.premier.net/~gero/geropsyc.html

Devoted to the study of the neurological, psychological, sociological aspects of the aging process. Designed for the gerontology professional, seniors, and caregivers, features and links are topically organized for quick reference.

Grand Times

http://www.grandtimes.com/

An online magazine for active retirees.

The John A. Hartford Foundation

http://www.jhartfound.org/

Founded in 1929, the John A. Hartford Foundation is a committed champion of health care training, research and service system innovations that will ensure the well-being and vitality of older adults. Its overall goal is to increase the nation's capacity to provide effective, affordable care to its rapidly increasing older population. Today, the Foundation is America's leading philanthropy with a sustained interest in aging and health.

Michigan Alzheimer's Disease Research Center

http://www.med.umich.edu/madrc/

Provides information about the activities of the MADRC, their research projects, publications, programs for patients and families, and links to other Alzheimer's centers and programs and resources.

National Council on Aging

http://www.ncoa.org/

An association of more than 7,500 members who work with, for, and on behalf of older persons. The organization is devoted "to promoting the dignity, self-determination, well-being, and contributions of older persons and to enhancing the field of aging through leadership and service, education, and advocacy . . . "

Senior Net

http://www.seniornet.org/

SeniorNet is a national nonprofit organization whose mission is to build a community of computer-using senior citizens. The site contains all kinds of information for and about seniors, instructional information on computing, and message boards and chat to enable seniors to contact each other.

Senior Sites

http://www.seniorsites.com/

This site may be the most comprehensive Web source of nonprofit housing and services for seniors. With over 5000 listed communities, Senior Sites is a valuable resource for seniors and their families interested in exploring the nonprofit housing option.

The University of Georgia Institute of Gerontology

http://www.geron.uga.edu/

Highlights the activities of the center, and provides links to other resources, including aging-related grants information.

The University of Utah Center on Aging

http://aging.utah.edu/

The Center on Aging provides the focal point uniting aging-related research, education, and clinical programs at the University of Utah. By linking its faculty and programs, the enter synergizes the growth and progress of interdisciplinary research to help people lead longer and more fulfilling lives and supports the development of multi-disciplinary clinical and training programs.

CHILDREN, ADOLESCENTS, AND FAMILIES

Adolescent Directory Online

http://education.indiana.edu/cas/adol/welcome.html

Adolescence Directory Online (ADOL) is an electronic guide to information on adolescent issues. It is a service of the Center for Adolescent Studies at Indiana University. Educators, counselors, parents, researchers, health practitioners, and teens can use ADOL to find Web resources on conflict and violence, mental health issues, health issues, counselor resources, and even help with homework.

American Academy of Child and Adolescent Psychiatry

http://www.aacap.org/

AACAP is a dynamic organization, giving direction to and responding quickly to new developments in health care, and addressing the needs of children, adolescents and families. Resources are provided to educate parents and families about psychiatric disorders affecting children and adolescents.

Casa de los Niños

http://www.casadelosninos.org/

The mission of Casa de los Niños is the prevention, intervention, and treatment of child abuse and neglect by providing: residential shelter care for children who are abused, neglected, or homeless; supportive counseling to families; and community education. The Web site features information about the organization, child abuse statistics, information for parents, and links to related resources.

Center for Adolescent Studies

http://www.indiana.edu/~cafs/

The Center for Adolescent Studies at Indiana University focuses on meeting the social and emotional growth and development needs of adolescents through providing support to adults working with youth, investigating current social issues and providing tools for teens to learn and practice new, healthy behaviors. Links are provided to Center programs, which include research projects, support for teachers, and a computer-based decision aide to help schools select the drug prevention program most likely to meet their needs.

Child Welfare

http://www.childwelfare.com/

Provides a gateway to information related to the welfare of children, and an electronic journal, Child Welfare Review, a library, a resource on issues related to sources on child welfare. It also features a directory of email addresses for social work faculty.

Child Welfare League of America

http://www.cwla.org/

The Child Welfare League of America is the nation's oldest and largest organization devoted entirely to the well-being of America's vulnerable children and their families. The site provides information about the CWLA, advocacy tips, action alerts, and child welfare statistics.

Children Now

http://www.childrennow.org/

Children Now is a nonpartisan, independent voice for children, working to translate the nation's commitment to children and families into action. The site provides access to Children Now publications, poll results, policy papers, press materials, action updates on federal and state legislation, and links to other Web sites devoted to children's issues. Users who subscribe to Children Now's Internet Digest receive online updates on children's issues.

Children's Defense Fund

http://www.childrensdefense.org/

The Children's Defense Fund exists to provide a strong and effective voice for all the children of America, who cannot vote, lobby, or speak for themselves. The site provides information about the activities of the CDF, issues, news and reports, the Black Community Crusade for Children, Stand for Children, and links to related resources.

Family.Com

`http://family.go.com/`

From Disney.com, Family.com is a service for parents offering comprehensive, high-quality, customizable information for raising children. Glitzy, but worth a visit.

National 4-H Council

`http://www.fourhcouncil.edu/`

National 4-H Council is a not-for-profit educational organization devoted to creating exciting programs and opportunities for young people. The site presents information about the organization and its activities.

National Network for Youth

`http://www.NN4Youth.org/`

The National Network for Youth informs public policy, educates the public and contributes to the field of youth work. The Web site provides information for youth work advocacy and links to other resources.

The State of the World's Children 2006

`http://www.unicef.org/sowc06/`

The State of the World's Children 2006: Excluded and Invisible is a sweeping assessment of the world's most vulnerable children, whose rights to a safe and healthy childhood are exceptionally difficult to protect. These children are growing up beyond the reach of development campaigns and are often invisible in everything from public debate and legislation, to statistics and news stories. UNICEF's award-winning site presents a snapshot of the world's children in 2006, including children in war, statistical tables, regional spotlights, and references.

YouthNet UK

http://www.thesite.org/

This UK site provides a wealth of information for youths about everything ranging from relationships to housing, and with links to virtually any subject that conceivably could be of interest to adolescents.

YO! Youth Outlook

http://www.youthoutlook.org

YO! Youth Outlook is an award-winning monthly publication by and for young people who have stories to share. Featuring in-depth reporting pieces and first-person essays, comic strips and poetry pages, YO! is the communication outlet for youths who feel their voice and visions need to be seen and heard. YO! is a bridge to the world of youth expression.

Youth and Children Resources Net

http://www.child.net/

Maintained by the National Children's Coalition with sponsorship from Streetcats Foundation, this page aspires to be a megasite. It provides links to news, information, resources and referrals for and about kids and teens on the World Wide Web.

CLINICAL SOCIAL WORK PRACTICE

APsa: The American Psychoanalytic Association

http://www.apsa.org/

Home page of the American Psychoanalytic Association.

Behaviour Analysis

http://psych.athabascau.ca/html/aupr/ba.shtml

Maintained by Athabasca University, this is believed to be the largest list of Web-based behavior-analysis resources on the Internet.

Behavior OnLine

http://www.behavior.net/

Behavior OnLine aspires to be the meeting place online for Mental Health and Applied Behavioral Science professionals. It hosts ongoing discussions on a variety of therapeutic approaches and provides links to organizations and interests groups and to other resources.

Counseling Center University at Buffalo

`http://ub-counseling.buffalo.edu/selfhelp.shtml`

The Counseling Center Self-Help Home Page presents a wide selection of documents, Internet resources, referrals, and reading lists, all to help students with day-to-day stresses and difficult periods in their lives.

The Gestalt Therapy Network

`http://www.gestalttherapy.net/`

The Gestalt Therapy Network is for the enrichment of Gestalt Therapy and for those who love it and practice it. Mental Health counselors, social workers, psychologists, psychotherapists, psychiatrists, lay analysts, students, trainees in mental health programs and those interested in the theory and practice of Gestalt therapy will benefit from a comprehensive Gestalt bibliography, a Directory of Gestalt Practitioners, links to Gestalt web sites, referrals, published and unpublished articles of interest to Gestalt practitioners, a Perls, Hefferline and Goodman book study group, and topic oriented weekend chat rooms. The Gestalt Therapy Network provides two online discussion Forums: The Theory and Practice of Gestalt Therapy for Gestalt practitioners and The Neighborhood, a place to share resources and communicate more informally.

Good Days Ahead: The Interactive Program for Depression and Anxiety

`http://mindstreet.com/`

MindStreet is a multimedia learning program which uses full-screen, full-motion video and consists of 5–8 hours of computer-assisted psychotherapy, plus a take-home manual with customized homework assignments for each patient. The program uses cognitive strategies for treating depression.

GrassRoots

`http://www.enabling.org/grassroots/`

GrassRoots is an online, text-based, virtual reality community, MOO, where people from around the world can come together for support, education, and fun. This online community is being designed to accommodate the needs of persons with disabilities. GrassRoots has been created in the Multi-user Object Oriented (MOO) programming language that has two components, allowing the creation of an accessible site that is uniquely effective for social interaction and education.

The National Institute for the Psychotherapies

http://www.nipinst.org/

The National Institute for the Psychotherapies (NIP) training programs enhance the capacity of mental health professionals to treat child, adolescent and adult clients. The training reflects a unique commitment to draw on a wide range of theories of psychotherapy, to support the integration of existing treatment modalities, and to develop new treatment approaches.

Practicing Psychotherapy on the Internet: Risk Management and Great Opportunity

http://telehealth.net/articles/njpa.html

Written by Marlene M. Maheu, Ph.D., discusses barriers to using the Internet for psychotherapy, including confidentiality, duty to warn dilemmas, and other concerns.

The Sigmund Freud Archives

http://www.freudarchives.org/

The Sigmund Freud Archives, Inc. is an entirely independent organization, founded in 1951. It is dedicated to collecting, conserving, collating and making available for scholarly use all of Sigmund Freud's psychoanalytic and personal papers, his correspondence, photos, records, memorabilia, etc. These documents are protected and preserved at the United States Library of Congress, in the Freud Collection, established with the collaboration and donation of Sigmund Freud Archives.

Support Coalition: Human Rights and Psychiatry Home Page

http://www.MindFreedom.org/

MindFreedom International unites 100 grassroots groups and thousands of members to win campaigns for human rights of people diagnosed with psychiatric disabilities. MindFreedom International is where mutual support meets human rights activism . . . and where democracy meets the mental health system.

COMMUNITY ORGANIZATIONS

Civic Practices Network

http://www.cpn.org

CPN is a collaborative and nonpartisan project bringing together a diverse array of organizations and perspectives within the citizen participation movement.

The Community Builders, Inc.

http://www.tcbinc.org/

The mission of The Community Builders, Inc. is to build strong communities where people of all incomes can achieve their full potential. They do this by developing, financing, and operating high quality affordable, mixed-income housing, by coordinating access to support services, and by planning and implementing other community and economic initiatives critical to the communities we serve. They focus primarily on meeting the needs of lower income people not effectively served by market forces. The Community Builders, Inc. works in collaboration with neighborhood groups, residents, public and private agencies, and philanthropic interests. Becoming a long-term stakeholder in the neighborhood, they create effective local implementation teams that combine neighborhood understanding, technical skills, and managerial ability.

Community Networking Documents and Resources

http://www.ifla.org/II/commun.htm

This site offers links to a variety of Internet resources related to Internet access and community-building.

The Digital Divide Network

http://www.digitaldividenetwork.org/

There has always been a gap between those people and communities who can make effective use of information technology and those who cannot. Now, more than ever, unequal adoption of technology excludes many from reaping the fruits of the economy. At the Digital Divide Network, the digital divide is examined from many perspectives. The Web site offers a range of information, tools and resources that help practitioners stay on top of digital divide developments. It also serves as forum where practitioners can share their experiences with colleagues around the world. They examine the causes and effects of the divide from four distinct angles: technology access, literacy and learning, content, and economic development.

HandsNet

http://www.handsnet.org/

HandsNet is a national, nonprofit organization that promotes information sharing, cross-sector collaboration and advocacy among individuals and organizations working on a broad range of public interest issues.

Idealist

http://www.idealist.org/

Idealist is a fully interactive system that enables any nonprofit or community organization—whether it has a Web site or not-to enter and update detailed information about its services, volunteer opportunities, internships, job openings, upcoming events, and any material or publication it has produced. 22,000 organizations in 150 countries are already using Idealist.

May First/People Link

http://mayfirst.org/

May First/People Link is an organization of progressive people who have joined together to improve access to the Internet, enhance its function as a tool for mass communication and organizing, develop new technologies and uses for it, and help social justice movements use it effectively to communicate with each other and with the world.

MoveOn.org

http://www.moveon.org/

MoveOn was started by Joan Blades and Wes Boyd, two Silicon Valley entrepreneurs, with their family and friends. MoveOn is working to bring ordinary people back into politics. Charging that the system today revolves around big money and big media, and that most citizens are left out. MoveOn is a catalyst for a new kind of grassroots involvement, supporting busy but concerned citizens in finding their political voice. MoveOn builds electronic advocacy groups around issues such as campaign finance, environmental and energy issues, impeachment, gun safety, and nuclear disarmament. MoveOn provides information and tools to help each individual have the greatest possible impact. During impeachment of President Clinton, for example, MoveOn's grassroots advocates generated more than 250,000 phone calls and a million emails to Congress.

National Urban League

`http://www.nul.org`

The mission of the National Urban League is to assist African Americans in the achievement of social and economic equality. The Board of Trustees of the National Urban League and all of its affiliates reflect a diverse body of community, government, and corporate leaders. The League implements its mission through advocacy, bridge building, program services, and research.

Neighborhoods Online

`http://neighborhoodsonline.net/`

Neighborhoods Online was created in 1995 by the Institute for the Study of Civic Values as an online resource center for people working to build strong communities throughout the United States. Their aim is to provide fast access to information and ideas covering all aspects of neighborhood revitalization, as well as to create a national network of neighborhood activists. The site offers information related to community development, education, crime, jobs, environment, health, and human services.

Smart Communities

`http://198.103.246.211/`

A Smart Community is a community with a vision of the future that involves the use of information and communication technologies in new and innovative ways to empower its residents, institutions and regions as a whole. As such, they make the most of the opportunities that new technologies afford—better health care delivery, better education and training and new business opportunities. The site profiles several models of smart communities.

Social Contract Project

`http://neighborhoodsonline.net/socialcontract.html`

Through the Social Contract Project, the Institute for the Study of Civic Values has developed a new way for neighborhood activists, business leaders, and public officials to develop comprehensive plans for neighborhood improvement. These stakeholders negotiate an explicit social contract defining how they will work together to make the neighborhood is clean, safe, economically viable, and a decent place to raise children. The site details the work of the project.

Time Dollar USA

http://www.timedollar.org/

Time Dollar USA seeks to build local economies and communities that reward decency, caring, and a passion for justice. Time Dollars are a time-based currency where one hour helping another earns one Time Dollar. With Time Dollars, everyone who gives can earn, and everyone has something to give. I help you, you help another, and that person helps another. Soon there is a web of caring, a new network of support. For those who are well-off as much as those who are poor, Time Dollars bring a new quality of community to daily living.

DISABILITIES

Ability

http://www.ability.org.uk/

Ability is a grassroots organization in the UK that is dedicated to utilizing computer technology and the Internet for people with disabilities. The site offers access to disability and health resources, social contacts, message boards, classified ads, and news.

Active Living Alliance

http://www.ala.ca/

The Active Living Alliance for Canadians with a Disability is a partnership of 17 National Associations whose common goal is to facilitate active living opportunities for Canadians with a disability. Information about the alliance, news, and links to related resources are offered.

The Kansas Commission on Disability Concerns

http://adabbs.hr.state.ks.us/dc/

This site offers a wealth of information and resources for people with disabilities in Kansas, nationally and internationally.

American Council of the Blind

http://www.acb.org/

This site offers information about the activities of the organization, recent issues of its monthly publications, and helpful resources and information about blindness.

American Foundation for the Blind

http://www.afb.org/

Information about the AFB, the *Journal of Visual Impairment and Blindness,* the AFB Press Catalog, the Helen Keller photograph collection, and information on blindness, low vision and related issues.

The Archimedes Project

http://archimedes.stanford.edu/

The mission of the Archimedes Project is to help secure equality of access to information for individuals with disabilities through the development of computer technology and the promulgation of knowledge about disability to present and future designers in academia and industry.

The ARC

http://TheArc.org

The Arc (formerly Association for Retarded Citizens of the United States) is the country's largest voluntary organization committed to the welfare of all children and adults with mental retardation and their families.

Assistive Technology, Inc.

http://www.assistivetech.com/

Assistive Technology, Inc. serves the disability and special education markets by providing innovative hardware and software solutions for people with special needs and the professionals who work with them.

Associated Services for the Blind

http://www.asb.org

This site offers information about the organization's services and information about subscribing to popular national magazines on cassette.

Attention Deficit Disorder Association

http://www.add.org/

The Attention Deficit Disorder Association (ADDA) has been in existence since 1989. The mission of ADDA is to provide information, resources and networking to adults with AD/HD and to the professionals who work with them. In doing so, ADDA generates hope, awareness, empowerment and connections worldwide in the field of AD/HD. Bringing together scientific perspectives and the human experience, the information and resources provided to individuals and families affected by AD/HD and professionals in the field focuses on diagnoses, treatments, strategies and techniques for helping adults with AD/HD lead better lives.

The British Dyslexia Association

http://www.bdadyslexia.org.uk/

The BDA sponsors the Dyslexia Archive, which is an ever-growing collection of up-to-date material covering all aspects of dyslexia.

The Center for Independent Living

http://www.cilberkeley.org/

The Center for Independent Living (CIL) is a national leader in helping people with disabilities live independently and become productive, fully participating members of society.

disABILITY Information and Resources

http://www.makoa.org/

One of the largest collections of resources for all types of disabilities.

Disabled Peoples' International

http://www.dpi.org

The purpose of DPI is to promote the Human Rights of People with Disabilities through full participation, equalization of opportunity and development. DPI is a grassroots, cross-disability network with member organizations in more than 120 countries, over half of which are in the developing world. DPI is administered through the headquarters in Winnipeg, Canada and through eight Regional Development Offices. DPI has consultative status with the ECOSOC,

UNESCO, WHO, and the ILO, and has official observer status at the United Nations General Assembly.

Down Syndrome WWW Page

http://www.nas.com/downsyn/

A support and information page for parents, professionals and others interested in Down syndrome.

ERIC Clearinghouse on Disabilities and Gifted Education

http://ericec.org

ERIC EC is part of the National Library of Education (NLE), Office of Educational Research and Improvement (OERI), U.S. Department of Education. It is operated by The Council for Exceptional Children (CEC). ERIC EC provides information on the education of individuals with disabilities as well as those who are gifted.

Gallaudet Research Institute

http://gri.gallaudet.edu/

Gallaudet University is the world's only four-year university for deaf and hard of hearing undergraduate students. The Gallaudet Research Institute specializes in research about the deaf.

Hattie Larlham Foundation

http://www.larlham.org/

HLF is a private, nonprofit service agency for young people with mental retardation, developmental disabilities and/or complex medical needs. The Web site is offered as a service for the families of children with profound disabilities, professionals who work with children having disabilities and anyone who wishes to learn more.

International Center for Disability Resources on the Internet

http://www.icdri.org/

The Center's mission is to collect and present as many disability-related Internet resources as there are available, including resources directly related to disabilities and other resources that may be helpful to the disability community. These resources are presented in a manner that is accessible to a wide and varied audience. The Center's scope is international.

LD OnLine

http://www.ldonline.org/

An interactive guide to learning disabilities for parents, teachers and children, LD OnLine offers links to resources, including research, information, referrals, bulletin boards, chats, and more.

National Federation of the Blind

http://www.nfb.org/

The goal of the NFB involves the removal of legal, economic, and social discriminations; the education of the public to new concepts concerning blindness; and the achievement by all blind people of the right to exercise to the fullest their individual talents and capacities.

National Library Service for the Blind and Physically Handicapped

http://www.loc.gov/nls/

The Library of Congress a free library program of Braille and recorded materials circulated to eligible borrowers through a network of cooperating libraries. This Web site offers access to online catalogs of holdings.

National Technical Institute for the Deaf

http://ntidweb.rit.edu/

One of the seven colleges of the Rochester Institute of Technology (RIT), NTID is the world's first and largest technological college for deaf students. It represents the first concerted effort to educate large numbers of deaf students within a college campus planned principally for hearing students.

SayWhatClub

http://www.saywhatclub.com/

SayWhatClub (SWC) is a non-profit internet based organization for people with hearing loss or interested in hearing loss issues. The Web site offers links to resources for people with hearing loss.

Shriver Center

http://www.umassmed.edu/shriver

The Eunice Kennedy Shriver Center for Mental Retardation, Inc. is a not-for-profit service, training and research institute. The site offers information about their research, training, and services divisions.

Values into Action

http://www.viauk.org/

VIA is a nonprofit organization that works to promote the rights of people with learning difficulties. The site offers information to promote the civil rights of people with disabilities.

DIVERSITY

Asian American Studies Resources

http://sun3.lib.uci.edu/~dtsang/aas2.htm

Provides a variety of links to Internet resources about Asian Americans.

Asian Studies WWW Monitor

http://coombs.anu.edu.au/asia-www-monitor.html

This online newsletter was established to provide resources that are inspected and rated in terms of the quality, overall reliability and usefulness of their content to the social sciences' research in Asia-Pacific region.

The Amistad Research Center

http://www.amistadresearchcenter.org/

An independent archives, library, and museum dedicated to preserving African-American and ethnic history and culture, housed at Tulane University.

The Center for Afroamerican and African Studies

http://www.umich.edu/~iinet/caas/

The Center for Afroamerican and African Studies (CAAS) at the University of Michigan functions as an academic department in the areas of African Studies, African American Studies, and Afro-Caribbean Studies. One of the few programs in the country to combine African Studies with the study of the people and cultures of the African diaspora, it has its own undergraduate program, courses, and faculty and is also home to the South African Initiatives Office and the African Studies Initiative Program. The site offers an Information Resource Center.

The Chicano/Latino Electronic Network

http://latino.sscnet.ucla.edu/

CLNet is an emerging digital library on Latinas/os in the United States and a joint project of the Center for Virtual Research in the College of Humanities, Arts, and Social Sciences at the UC Riverside, the Chicano Studies Research Library at UCLA and the Linguistic Minority Research Institute at the UC Santa Barbara.

The Cradleboard Teaching Project

http://www.cradleboard.org/

Founded by Buffy Sainte-Marie, the Nihewan Foundation is dedicated to the development of curricula for American Indian Education. Included in this site is a comprehensive listing of links to Tribal resources across North America.

Institute of Hispanic-Latino Cultures

http://www.dso.ufl.edu/multicultural/lacasita/

Offers information for students at the University of Florida.

LATIF.com Home

http://www.latif.com/links/

A listing of links and informational resources about Islam.

Latin-American Network Information Center

http://info.lanic.utexas.edu/

This site is considered by some to be by far the best online resource for information about Latin America and the Caribbean.

Minority Rights Group International

http://www.minorityrights.org/

MRG is an international non-governmental organization working to secure justice for minorities and majorities suffering discrimination and prejudice and to active the peaceful coexistence of majority and minority communities. MRG informs and warns governments, the international community, non-governmental organizations and the wider public about the situation of minorities around the world.

Native American Resources

http://www.cowboy.net/native/

An abundance of links to Indian-focused Internet resources, including Tribes, Indian organizations, education, government, and art and culture.

Swagga.Com

http://www.swagga.com/

This site represents a compendium of links to Internet resources for African Americans.

Tribal and Inter-Tribal Resolutions and Papers

http://www.cwis.org/resolutions.html

Sponsored by the Center For World Indigenous Studies and the Fourth World Documentation Project. This project is an online library of texts that record and preserve Indian struggles to regain their rightful place in the international community.

UCI Southeast Asian Archive

http://www.lib.uci.edu/libraries/collections/
sea/sasian.html

The Archive, housed at University of California, Irvine Libraries, collects materials relating to the resettlement of Southeast Asian refugees and immigrants in the United States, the "boat people" and land refugees, and the culture and history of Cambodia, Laos, and Vietnam.

The UCLA Asian American Studies Center

http://www.aasc.ucla.edu/

Highlights the activities of the center, provides access to publications, and links to related resources.

The WWW Hmong Home Page

http://www.hmongnet.org

The WWW Hmong Home Page, first made available on the Internet in March, 1994, is a volunteer effort bringing together a collection the Internet-based resources related to Hmong news and current-events, issues, history, publications, and culture. This site is an official Asian Studies WWW Virtual Library Associate site.

GENDER

Bookbeast's Feminist Threads Home Page

http://www.bookbeast.com/ft.htm

Offers a variety of information of interest to women, including eco-feminism, ethnic and international resources, U.S. Politics, general and reference resources, books and publications, law and freedom, religion, lesbian culture, music, art and film, health and safety, work and leisure, and notices about upcoming events.

Feminist.Com

http://feminist.com/

FEMINIST.COM is aimed at helping women network, and educating and empowering women (and men) on issues that affect their lives. Offers news, information about resources, activism, women's health, articles and speeches, women-owned businesses, and classifieds.

Feminist Majority Foundation

http://www.feminist.org/

The Feminist Majority and The Feminist Majority Foundation are committed to empowering women and winning equality through research, the sharing of information of value to feminists everywhere, and effective action. The site offers action alerts, news and press releases, and information about events of interest.

Feminist Theory Web Site

http://www.cddc.vt.edu/feminism/

The Feminist Theory Web site provides research materials and information for students, activists, and scholars interested in women's conditions and struggles around the world. The goals of this Web site are: 1) to encourage a wide range of research into feminist theory, and 2) to encourage dialogue between women (and men) from different countries around the world. Hopefully, this will result in new connections, new ideas, and new information about feminist theory and women's movements.

The International Foundation for Gender Education

http://www.ifge.org/

The International Foundation for Gender Education (IFGE), founded in 1987, is a leading advocate and educational organization for promoting the self-definition and free expression of individual gender identity.

Men's Movement Resources on the Web

`http://www.psychstat.missouristate.edu/scripts/dws148f/mensresourcesmain.asp`

David W. Stockburger has compiled a list of resources for men's issues, including organizations, literature and information, advocacy pages, and government links.

MenWeb

`http://www.menweb.org/`

MenWeb men's issues site covers mythopoetic men's movement, psychology, therapy, healing, men's rights, and gender justice. The site includes men's stories, book reviews, RealAudio WebCasts, poems, and an online book store.

National Organization for Women

`http://now.org/`

Official home page of the National Organization for Women. Offers information about the organization and its agenda, as well as feminism, women, abortion rights, violence against women, racial and ethnic diversity, and economic equity.

Women's Resource Center

`http://www.Colorado.edu/StudentAffairs/WomensResourceCenter/`

The Women's Resource Center at the University of Colorado, Boulder serves as a resource for the university community and an advocate for women of all backgrounds, races, classes, ages, sexual orientations, political and religious beliefs, and physical abilities.

Women's Resources on the Web

`http://www.dsiegel.com/women/index.html`

Offers links related to health, safety, sexuality, sports, Women's Studies, women in technology, politics and activism, and more.

Women's Studies (R)E-sources on the Web

http://scriptorium.lib.duke.edu/women/cyber.html

Lots of women's studies links. The various Internet sites listed are primarily electronic sources that may be useful for Women's Studies.

WWWomen!

http://www.wwwomen.com/

Considered to be the premier search directory for women's resources on the Internet, offers both hierarchical and keyword searching.

HEALTH

American Public Health Association

http://www.apha.org/

APHA represents more than 50,000 members from over 50 occupations of public health, bringing together researchers, health service providers, administrators, teachers, and other health workers in a unique, multidisciplinary environment of professional exchange, study, and action.

The Canadian Health Network

http://www.hc-sc.gc.ca/

Information about the health care system in Canada and links to informational resources.

CancerWEB

http://cancerweb.ncl.ac.uk/

This cancer resource site has information available on many different aspects of cancer investigation and treatment. Especially helpful is an online medical dictionary.

Center for Rural Health and Social Service Development

http://www.siu.edu/~crhssd/

Southern Illinois University at Carbondale's CRHSSD conducts research, needs assessments, demonstration projects, program evaluations, and training; tests new models of health care delivery; and develops policy recommendations to improve the health of our rural population.

ChronicILLNet

http://www.chronicillnet.org/

This is the first multimedia information source on the Internet dedicated to chronic illnesses including AIDS, cancer, Gulf War Syndrome, autoimmune diseases, Chronic Fatigue Syndrome, heart disease and neurological diseases. This site offers information for researchers, patients, lay people, and physicians.

Clinical Trials Listings

http://www.CenterWatch.com/

Center Watch is a publishing company that focuses on the clinical trials industry. Their Web site is dedicated to assisting patients and their advocates to learn about and identify ongoing clinical trials seeking study volunteers.

The Cochrane Collaboration

http://www.cochrane.org

The Cochrane Collaboration is an international non-profit and independent organization, dedicated to making up-to-date, accurate information about the effects of healthcare readily available worldwide. It produces and disseminates systematic reviews of healthcare interventions and promotes the search for evidence in the form of clinical trials and other studies of interventions. The Cochrane Collaboration was founded in 1993 and named for the British epidemiologist, Archie Cochrane.

Cochrane Collaboration Consumer Network

http://www.cochrane.org/consumers/homepage.htm

The Cochrane Consumer Network is made up of fellow consumers who are committed to the philosophies of The Cochrane Collaboration and the importance of consumer participation in informed healthcare decision-making processes.

Diabetes Public Health Resources

http://www.cdc.gov/diabetes/

Sponsored by the Division of Diabetes Translation, a division of the National Center for Chronic Disease Prevention and Health Promotion of the Centers for Disease Control and Prevention. The division is responsible for translating scientific research findings into health promotion, disease prevention and treatment strategies.

GeneralPediatrics.com

http://www.generalpediatrics.com/

GeneralPediatrics.com is curated and maintained by Donna M. D'Alessandro, M.D. It consists of a wealth of links to pediatric resources on the World Wide Web.

Go Ask Alice!

http://www.goaskalice.columbia.edu/

Sponsored by Healthwise, the Health Education and Wellness program of the Columbia University Health Service, *Go Ask Alice!* is an interactive question and answer service, answering questions each week about health, including questions about sexuality, sexual health, relationships, general health, fitness and nutrition, emotional well-being, and alcohol and other drugs.

The Health Care for the Homeless Information Resource Center

http://www.bphc.hrsa.gov/hchirc/

The Health Care for the Homeless Information Resource Center offers front-line providers and program staff easy access to the most current research and information about clinical practices, funding opportunities, and legislative initiatives that impact their work. Operated for the Health Resources and Services Administration's Bureau of Primary Health Care by Policy Research Associates, Inc., the Health Care for the Homeless Information Resource Center supports the effective delivery of health care services to homeless people by providing technical assistance and targeted information.

Healthfinder®

http://www.healthfinder.gov/

Healthfinder® is a gateway consumer health and human services information Web site from the United States government. Healthfinder® can lead you to selected online publications, clearinghouses, databases, Web sites, and support and self-help groups, as well as the government agencies and not-for-profit organizations that produce reliable information for the public. Launched in April 1997, Healthfinder® served Internet users over 1.7 million times in its first year online.

Juvenile Diabetes Foundation

http://www.jdf.org/

The Juvenile Diabetes Foundation is a not-for-profit, voluntary health agency whose mission is to support and fund research to find a cure for diabetes and its complications. The site offers a range of diabetes information.

Med Help International

http://www.medhelp.org/

Med Help International is dedicated to helping all who are in need find qualified medical information and support for their medical conditions and questions, regardless of their economic status or geographic location. Offers library searches and patient support through chat resources.

MedlinePlus: Drugs & Supplements

http://www.nlm.nih.gov/medlineplus/
druginformation.html

MedlinePlus will direct you to information to help answer health questions. MedlinePlus brings together authoritative information from NLM, the National Institutes of Health (NIH), and other government agencies and health-related organizations. Preformulated MEDLINE searches are included in MedlinePlus and give easy access to medical journal articles. MedlinePlus also has extensive information about drugs, an illustrated medical encyclopedia, interactive patient tutorials, and latest health news.

The Minority Health Network

http://www.pitt.edu/AFShome/e/j/ejb4/public/
html/min

MHNet is a World Wide Web based information source for individuals interested in the health of minority groups, referring to all people of color and people who are underrepresented economically and socially.

Muscular Dystrophy Association

http://www.mdausa.org/

Offers links to information about MD and to related associations worldwide.

National Center for Farmworker Health

http://www.ncfh.org/

NCFH is a private, not-for-profit corporation located in Austin, Texas. NCFH has evolved into a multi-faceted organization that provides a wide range of services dedicated to improving the health of the workers who harvest America's crops.

National Center for Health Education

http://www.nche.org/

The National Center for Health Education (NCHE) is a nonprofit health education organization. We design and disseminate health education programs including *Growing Healthy,* America's first comprehensive school health education curriculum. *Growing Healthy* is designed to provide teachers of school health education with the tools needed to effectively teach health education. We also develop health education products that cover topics including violence prevention, drug prevention, and adolescent health issues including HIV and AIDS, sexuality education, sexually transmitted diseases (STDs), sexual abuse, and birth control and unintended pregnancy.

Nursing Net

http://www.nursingnet.org/

NursingNet's mission is to help further the knowledge and understanding of Nursing for the public, and to provide a forum for medical professionals and students to obtain and disseminate information about nursing and medically related subjects. Offers a wide range of Internet nursing resources.

Online Diabetes Resources

http://www.mendosa.com/faq.htm

This comprehensive directory of substantive information about diabetes provides links to important resources for diabetics.

National Information Center on Health Services Research & Health Care Technology

http://www.nlm.nih.gov/nichsr/

NICHSR was created at the National Library of to improve the collection, storage, analysis, retrieval, and dissemination of information on health services research, clinical practice guidelines, and on health care technology, including the assessment of such technology.

WWW Virtual Library: Biosciences: Medicine

http://www.ohsu.edu/cliniweb/wwwvl/

An hierarchical listing of medical topics for finding resources on the Web.

Y-Me National Breast Cancer Organization

http://www.y-me.org/

Y-ME National Breast Cancer Organization has a commitment to provide information and support to anyone who has been touched by breast cancer. Y-ME serves women with breast cancer and their families and friends through their national hotline, open door groups, early detection workshops and local chapters.

HIV/AIDS

ACT-UP NY

http://www.actupny.org/

The New York chapter of this advocacy and political action group's home page provides information about the organization, links, and an activist email list signup.

AIDSmap

http://www.aidsmap.com

A very useful gateway to HIV and AIDS related information for the UK.

AIDS Project—Los Angeles

http://www.apla.org/

Uses a search engine to link users to a variety of information, including services, special events, volunteer opportunities, publications, grass roots organizing, and information links.

AIDS Resource List

http://www.specialweb.com/aids/

A comprehensive list of HIV/AIDS related links from Celine Chamberlin, a self-proclaimed Internet addict.

The Body: A Multimedia AIDS and HIV Resource

http://www.thebody.com/

Covers many topics, including: prevention, safe sex, testing, treatment (protease inhibitors, combination therapy, viral load, azt, ddi, ddc, d4t, 3tc, reverse transcriptase), QandA w/ experts, hotlines, and politics.

Center for AIDS Prevention Studies

http://www.caps.ucsf.edu/

CAPS is committed to maintaining a focus on prevention of HIV disease, using the expertise of multiple disciplines, and an applied and community-based perspective within a university setting. The Web site features information about the activities of the center, fact sheets, and a "Prevention Toolbox."

Children with AIDS Project

http://www.aidskids.org/

Children with AIDS Project of America offers a variety of services for children infected/affected by AIDS or drug exposed infants who will require foster or adoptive families. The site offers information about the organization and links to other resources.

Critical Path AIDS Project

http://www.critpath.org/

The Critical Path AIDS Project was founded by persons with AIDS to provide treatment, resource and prevention information for researchers, service providers, treatment activists, but primarily for other persons with AIDS.

Detroit Community AIDS Library

http://www.lib.wayne.edu/dcal/

Gateway to HIV/AIDS Information for Detroit and Southeastern Michigan. Provides links to news and announcements, local AIDS service organizations, searchable databases, and HIV/AIDS Internet resources.

Health and Law Policy Institute

http://www.law.uh.edu/healthlaw/

Several papers on legal issues relating to HIV and AIDS from the University of Houston Law Center.

HIV InSite

`http://hivinsite.ucsf.edu/`

Comprehensive and reliable information on HIV/AIDS treatment, policy, research, epidemiology, and prevention from the University of California, San Francisco.

HIV Law: Paul Hampton Crockett

`http://www.thebody.com/crockett/legalix.html`

Paul Hampton Crockett is a partner in the law firm of Crockett & Chasen, P.A. in South Miami Beach. He and his partner specialize in the legal advice and representation of gays and lesbians, and also specialize in the large number of legal issues raised by HIV, including estate and health care planning, disability planning, insurance issues, viatical settlements, and the law of discrimination. He has served as a volunteer for ten years with the Health Crisis Network, a community-based comprehensive AIDS services organization in Dade County, Florida, and currently sits on the organization's board of directors. This site links to a number of pages written by him about HIV law, which represent a comprehensive survival guide to the legal system for people living with HIV.

HIVpositive.com

`http://www.hivpositive.com/`

The HIVpositive site offers HIV-related info on a wide-range of topics including but not limited to nutrition, treatment, caregivers, finances, and drug advisories. The mission of the site is to improve the quality of life of anyone affected in some way by the HIV virus. Among the agencies contributing information are the CDC, FDA, NIH, the Gay Men's Health Crisis, and the American Foundation for AIDS Research.

HIV/AIDS Treatment Information

`http://www.hivatis.org/`

The HIV/AIDS Treatment Information Service (ATIS) provides timely, accurate treatment information on HIV and AIDS through the use of federally approved treatment guidelines and information. The HSTAT database contains the full text of approved treatment guidelines being used by the service.

International Council of AIDS Service Organizations

http://www.icaso.org/

The ICASO network is an interactive global focus point in the international HIV/AIDS world, gathering and disseminating information and analysis on key issues, coordinating the development of CBO/NGO positions on these issues, and working as partners with key international agencies to ensure that the concerns and interests of CBOs and NGOs around the world are articulated and represented at all levels.

Medscape—AIDS

http://www.medscape.com/Home/Topics/AIDS/AIDS.html

Medscape features peer-reviewed articles, zoomable color graphics, self-assessment features, medical information, medical news, free MEDLINE, CME credit, and annotated links to Internet resources.

National Centre in HIV Social Research

http://nchsr.arts.unsw.edu.au/

The site documents the research activities of this Australian center.

Pets Are Loving Support

http://www.sonic.net/~pals/

PALS is a nonprofit agency organized to improve the quality of life of people with AIDS by preserving and promoting the human/animal bond through the care and maintenance of their animal companions.

SWEAIDS-NET

http://www.mun.ca/sweaids/sweaids.html

HIV/AIDS Social Work Education Canadian Network. The site serves as an interactive tool for sharing experiences, resources, and information social work educators, field instructors, students and trainers involved in HIV/AIDS related social work.

UNAIDS

http://www.unaids.org/

The Joint United Nations Programme on HIV/AIDS maintains this page to disseminate information on HIV/AIDS.

www.aidsnyc.org

http://www.aidsnyc.org/

A linked collection of pages from HIV/AIDS community-based organizations in New York City.

HOUSING, HUNGER, AND POVERTY

Action Aid

http://www.actionaid.org/

ACTIONAID is a leading development charity working directly with three million of the world's poorest people in Africa, Asia and Latin America, helping them in their fight against poverty.

America's Charities

http://www.charities.org/

America's Charities goal is to provide member charities with the necessary resources to meet needs impacting human service, health and education, civil and human rights, and the environment.

Bread for the World

http://www.bread.org/

Citizens' movement seeking justice for the world's hungry people by lobbying our nation's decision-makers.

Food For The Hungry: World Crisis Network

http://www.fh.org/

Food for the Hungry feeds the hungry worldwide. The site provides information about hunger and connects volunteers with sponsorship activities.

Food Research and Action Center

http://www.frac.org/

FRAC works to improve public policies to eradicate hunger and under nutrition in the United States.

HomeAid America

http://www.HomeAid.org/

HomeAid's mission is to build or renovate shelters for transitionally homeless men, women and children. HomeAid was created to help National Association of Home Builders—affiliated home building associations develop their own independently operated HomeAid programs to help fulfill the HomeAid mission across the nation. The Orange County site offers links to several housing-related information resources.

Homeless in America

http://www.homelessinamerica.org/

Homeless In America is a non-profit organization dedicated to providing safe and secure housing on a temporary basis for homeless families with children while working their way back and providing them with a fresh start in life.

Homelessness

http://aspe.hhs.gov/homeless/index.shtml

Offers information about homelessness in America as well as about U.S. Department of Health and Human Services assistance programs, publications, research results, and other resources.

Hunger Notes

http://www.worldhunger.org/

Hunger Notes is an online journal sponsored by the World Hunger Education Service. Its mission is to inform the community of people interested in issues of hunger and poverty, the public, and policymakers, about the causes, extent, and efforts to end hunger and poverty in the United States and the world; to promote further understanding which integrates ethical, religious, social, economic, political, and scientific perspectives on hunger and poverty; to facilitate communication and networking among those who are working for solutions; and to promote individual and collective commitment to solutions to the hunger and poverty which confront hundreds of millions of the people of the world.

HungerWeb

http://nutrition.tufts.edu/academic/hungerweb/

A project of the World Hunger Program, HungerWeb aims to help prevent and eradicate hunger by facilitating the free exchange of ideas and information regarding the causes of, and solutions to, hunger.

Institute for Research on Poverty (IRP)

http://www.irp.wisc.edu/

IRP provides online publications and extensive links to poverty-related statistics and information sources.

Joint Center for Poverty Research

http://www.jcpr.org/

The Northwestern University /University of Chicago Joint Center for Poverty Research is a national and interdisciplinary community of researchers whose work advances the understanding of what it means to be poor and live in America.

Luxembourg Income Study

http://www.lisproject.org/

The Luxembourg Income Study is a non-profit cooperative research project with a membership that includes 30 countries on four continents: Europe, America, Asia and Oceania. The LIS project began in 1983 under the joint sponsorship of the government of the Grand Duchy of Luxembourg and the Centre for Population, Poverty and Policy Studies (CEPS). The project is mainly funded by the national science and social science research foundations of its member countries. Recently, LIS and the University of Luxembourg became partners, with offices being provided by the university.

National Center for Children in Poverty

http://www.nccp.org/

The mission of the National Center for Children in Poverty is to identify and promote strategies that reduce the number of young children living in poverty in the United States, and that improve the life chances of the millions of children under six who are growing up poor. Center projects concentrate on early childhood care and education; child and family health; family and community support; crosscutting, multistate policy analyses; demographic and evaluation research; and communications.

National Association for the Education of Homeless Children and Youth

http://www.naehcy.org

NAEHCY, a national grassroots membership association, serves as the voice and the social conscience for the education of children and youth in homeless situations. NAEHCY connects educators, parents, advocates, researchers and service providers to ensure school academic achievement and overall success for children and youth whose lives have been disrupted by the lack of safe, permanent and adequate housing. NAEHCY accomplishes these goals through advocacy, partnerships and education.

National Coalition for the Homeless

http://www.nationalhomeless.org/

The National Coalition for the Homeless is a national advocacy network of homeless persons, activists, service providers, and others committed to ending homelessness through public education, policy advocacy, grassroots organizing, and technical assistance.

National Health Care for the Homeless Council, Inc.

http://www.nhchc.org/

Membership organization of health care providers working to help bring about reform of the health care system to best serve the needs of people who are homeless.

Northwest Harvest

http://www.northwestharvest.org/

Northwest Harvest collects and distributes food to approximately 280 hunger programs in Washington State without tax dollars or fees of any kind. In an average month, 500,000 services are provided to individuals and families in need. Nearly half of these services go to children.

Poverty Reduction

http://www.undp.org/poverty/

Through the Millennium Development Goals the world is addressing the many dimensions of human development, including halving by 2015 the proportion of people living in extreme poverty. Developing countries are working to create their own national poverty eradication strategies based on local needs and priorities. UNDP advocates for these nationally-owned solutions and helps to make them effective through ensuring a greater voice for poor people, expanding access to productive assets and economic opportunities, and linking poverty programs with countries' international economic and financial policies. At the same time, UNDP contributes to efforts at reforming trade, debt relief and investment arrangements to better support national poverty reduction and make globalization work for poor people. In doing so, we sponsor innovative pilot projects; connect countries to global best practices and resources; promote the role of women in development; and bring governments, civil society and outside funders together to coordinate their efforts.

Real Change

http://www.realchangenews.org/

The Real Change Homeless Empowerment Project has many faces, a newspaper, an advocacy group, a Homeless Speakers Bureau, and literary workshops. We do a lot, and all of it is working toward building bridges among the poor, homeless and the greater community, while engaging the broader public in fighting for economic justice. By publishing the newspaper and mobilizing the public around poverty issues, Real Change organizes, educates and builds alliances to find community-based solutions to homelessness and poverty.

RESULTS: Creating Political Will to End Hunger

http://www.resultsusa.org

RESULTS is a nonprofit, grassroots citizen's lobby that identifies sustainable solutions to the problems of hunger and poverty, nationally and worldwide, and works to generate the resources necessary to make those solutions succeed. The site features information about the organization, action alerts, background on hunger and poverty issues, Capitol updates, articles about the organization, and links to other Web sites.

World Hunger Year

http://www.worldhungeryear.org/

Founded by Harry Chapin in 1975, WHY focuses attention on hunger and poverty and the grassroots initiatives that fight them.

MENTAL HEALTH

At Health Home Page

http://www.athealth.com/

At Health provides mental health information, resources, a directory of licensed psychiatrists, psychologists, counselors and other therapists, and continuing education information.

Autism/PDD Resources Network

http://www.autism-pdd.net/

The purpose of the site is to guide users to key issues associated with Autism Spectrum disorders.

Center for Mental Health Services

http://www.mentalhealth.samhsa.gov/cmhs/

The Center for Mental Health Services (CMHS) leads Federal efforts to treat mental illnesses by promoting mental health and by preventing the development or worsening of mental illness when possible. CMHS was established under the 1992 ADAMHA Reorganization Act, Public Law 102-321, which mandates CMHS' leadership role in delivering mental health services, generating and applying new knowledge, and establishing national mental health policy. CMHS is a component of the Substance Abuse and Mental Health Services Administration, U.S. Department of Health and Human Services.

Children and Adults with Attention Deficit Disorder

http://www.chadd.org/

C.H.A.D.D. is a nonprofit parent-based organization formed to better the lives of individuals with attention deficit disorders and those who care for them through family support and advocacy, public and professional education and encouragement of scientific research.

Crisis, Grief, and Healing

http://www.webhealing.com/

This page is meant to be a place men and women can browse to understand and honor the many different paths to heal strong emotions.

David Baldwin's Trauma Information Pages

http://www.trauma-pages.com/

The Trauma Information Pages focus primarily on emotional trauma and traumatic stress, including PTSD (Post-traumatic Stress Disorder), whether following individual traumatic experience(s) or a large-scale disaster. New information is added to this site about once a month. The purpose of this award-winning site is to provide information about traumatic stress for clinicians and researchers in the field.

Dr. Grohol's Mental Health Page

http://psychcentral.com/

Extensive collection of articles, commentaries, and lists pertaining to mental health, for those interested in psychological self-help. Includes original articles and editorials on current issues in the field, consumer-oriented advice.

False Memory Syndrome Facts

http://fmsf.com/

This site offers pointers to key resources about "false memory syndrome," dissociation, delayed recall, repression, and recovered memories of child abuse and other traumatic events.

Memory and Reality: The False Memory Syndrome Foundation

http://www.fmsfonline.org/

The FMS Foundation is a nonprofit organization that is devoted to seeking the reasons for the spread of False Memory Syndrome; to working for the prevention of new cases of False Memory Syndrome; and to aiding the victims, both primary and secondary, of False Memory Syndrome.

GriefNet

http://www.griefnet.org

Bereavement, grief, death and dying resources.

Institute of Psychiatry Library: Mental Health

http://www.iop.kcl.ac.uk/iopweb/departments/home/default.aspx?locator=12

A very comprehensive list of links to resources in mental health.

The International Society for Mental Health Online

http://www.ismho.org/

The International Society for Mental Health Online (ISMHO) was formed in 1997 to promote the understanding, use and development of online communication, information and technology for the international mental health community.

Louis de la Parte Florida Mental Health Institute

http://home.fmhi.usf.edu/

The state's primary research and training center for mental health services is recognized nationally for its innovative research and training. The site offers information about mental health needs and services in the state of Florida, and links to relevant information, including electronic publications.

MedlinePlus: Bereavement

http://www.nlm.nih.gov/medlineplus/bereavement.html

An up-to-date set of links to resources for mourners.

Mental Health Matters!

http://www.mental-health-matters.com/

Mental Health Matters! is a directory of mental health and mental illness information and resources for mental health professionals, patients, and families.

Mental Health Net

http://mentalhelp.net/

MHN considers itself the largest, most comprehensive guide to mental health online, featuring over 7,000 individual resources. This site, winner of several awards, covers information on disorders such as depression, anxiety, panic attacks, chronic fatigue syndrome and substance abuse, to professional resources in psychology, psychiatry and social work, journals, and self-help magazines.

Mental Health Resources for Consumers and Professionals

http://mentalhealth.about.com/

About.com has developed more than 700 World Wide Web guides in a variety of topical areas. The Mental Health guide was developed by Leonard Holmes, a clinical psychologist in private practice who also provides mental health services over the Net. The site provides links to an impressive variety of informational resources for mental health.

National Alliance for the Mentally Ill

http://www.nami.org/

Grassroots, self-help organization of people with serious mental illness and their families and friends. NAMI's mission is to eradicate mental illness and to improve the quality of life for those who have mental illness.

National Center for PTSD

http://www.ncptsd.va.gov/

U.S. Department of Veterans Affairs National Center for PTSD offers research and education on Post-Traumatic Stress Disorder.

National Institute of Mental Health

http://www.nimh.nih.gov/

General information about NIMH, public information about mental health, including videos, news and announcements from NIMH, grants, contracts, and committee information, and information on NIMH research activities.

National Mental Health Association

http://www.nmha.org/

The National Mental Health Association, through its national office and more than 300 affiliates nationwide, is dedicated to improving the mental health of all individuals and achieving victory over mental illnesses.

Post Traumatic Stress Disorder Links

http://www.lawandpsychiatry.com/html/ptsdlinks.htm

A list of excellent links from Mark Levy, MD, who specializes in forensic psychiatry.

Psychiatry Online

http://www.priory.co.uk/psych.htm

The International Forum for Psychiatry—a peer reviewed, independent psychiatry journal for psychiatrists and mental health professionals. Contains articles, archives, and links to professional resources.

SAMHSA's National Mental Health Information Center

http://www.mentalhealth.samhsa.gov/cmhs/

The Center for Mental Health Services (CMHS) is the Federal agency within the U.S. Substance Abuse and Mental Health Services

Administration (SAMHSA) that leads national efforts to improve prevention and mental health treatment services for all Americans. CMHS pursues its mission by helping States improve and increase the quality and range of treatment, rehabilitation, and support services for people with mental health problems, their families, and communities. The Web site points to information about SAMHSA programs, mental health topics, news briefings, publications, and links to resources.

Specifica Mental Health Resources

http://www.realtime.net/~mmjw/

A topical list of references for consumers by Jeanine Wade, Ph.D.

Stress Free NET

http://www.stressfree.com/

StressFree Net offers stress related services and tools, including a directory of health and stress management professionals to help the user, and an opportunity to "Ask the Psychologist."

Screening for Suicide Risk

http://cpmcnet.columbia.edu/texts/gcps/gcps0060.html

Important information on screening for suicide intent from Columbia-Presbyterian Medical Center.

UCLA School Mental Health Project

http://smhp.psych.ucla.edu/

The School Mental Health Project (SMHP) was created to pursue theory, research, practice and training related to meeting the mental health needs of youngsters through school-based interventions. Their award winning Web site offers information on our clearinghouse, introductory packets, consultation cadre, newsletter, links to other Internet sites and electronic networking.

The Wounded Healer Journal

http://twhj.com/

Issues of grief and loss for survivors of sexual abuse.

POLICY PRACTICE

NOW and Welfare

http://now.org/issues/economic/welfare/

The National Organization for Women presents a policy analysis relating welfare reform and domestic violence.

Behaviorists for Social Responsibility

http://www.bfsr.org/

BFSR is a Special Interest Group of the Association for Behavior Analysis. The SIG and the site are dedicated to applications of the science of behavior and cultural analysis to issues of social importance, including education, human rights, environmental, and social justice issues. The site includes links to related state-of-the art publications and related sites.

Canadian Centre for Policy Alternatives

http://www.policyalternatives.ca/

The Canadian Centre for Policy Alternatives was founded in 1980 to promote research on economic and social issues facing Canada. The Centre monitors current developments in the economy and studies important trends that affect Canadians. The Web site provides information about the activities of the center, its publications and links to related resources.

Canadian Council on Social Development

http://www.ccsd.ca/

The Canadian Council on Social Development is a voluntary, non-profit organization whose mission is to develop and promote progressive social policies inspired by social justice, equality and the empowerment of individuals and communities through research, consultation, public education and advocacy. The Web site features information about the center and access to its statistical databases.

Centre for Social Policy Research and Development

http://www.bangor.ac.uk/csprd/

The Centre for Social Policy Research and Development (CSPRD) at the University of Wales, Bangor, is committed to the conduct of well-founded, scientific research primarily in the areas of human development, health studies and social care provision. The site offers information about the center, research reports, and links to related resources.

The Century Foundation

http://www.tcf.org/

The Century Foundation is a nonprofit public policy research institution that produces publications and convenes events that explain and analysis public issues in plain language, provide facts and opinions about the strengths and weaknesses of different policy strategies, and develop and call attention to distinctive ideas that can work. Their efforts are wide-ranging but focus particularly on four broad domestic and international challenges facing the United States: rising economic inequality combined with the shift to American households of financial risks previously borne by employers and government; the aging of the population; preventing and responding to terrorism while preserving civil liberties; and restoring America's international credibility as an effective and cooperative leader in responding to global security and economic dangers.

Congress Merge

http://www.congressmerge.com/

Congress Merge uses technology to assist legislative/congressional lobbying and advocacy efforts. Congress Merge provides tables linking zip codes to congressional and/or state legislative districts as well as tables with legislator contact information, committee assignments, biographies and district offices.

Congress.org—A Guide to the U.S. Congress

http://congress.org/

Congress.org is an updated online directory of information for both the US House of Representatives and the US Senate. A comprehensive resource for communicating with Congress, the structure and features of Congress.org can be customized to the needs of any organization or business involved in public affairs or grassroots activities.

Contacting the Congress

http://www.visi.com/juan/congress/

Contacting the Congress is a very up-to-date database of congressional contact information for the 109th Congress. As of June 16, 2006 there are 537 email addresses (of which 490 are Web-based email homepages), and 537 WWW homepages known for the 540 members of the 109th Congress. More traditional ground mail addresses are available for all Congressmembers.

Federal News Service

http://www.fnsg.com/

FNS allows you to read the actual words spoken by national leaders on matters of official U.S. Government policy and other issues of the day, the same day.

The Lindesmith Center—Drug Policy Foundation

http://www.lindesmith.org/

The Lindesmith Center—Drug Policy Foundation is a drug policy organization working to broaden and better inform the public debate on drug policy and related issues. The Lindesmith Center, created in 1994, is the leading independent drug policy institute in the United States.

PoliticsOnline

http://www.politicsonline.com/

This site is devoted to providing tools, tips and news about how to use the Internet to make political communications more effective.

PRAXIS

http://www.sp2.upenn.edu/~restes/praxis.html

The international development home page of Prof. Richard J. Estes of the University of Pennsylvania, this site to an array of archival resources on international and comparative social development designed to meet the informational needs of social work educators and students with international interests and other educators and students who require assistance in locating useful national and international resources on social and economic development.

Project Vote Smart

http://www.vote-smart.org/

Project Vote Smart tracks the performance of over 13,000 political leaders, including the President, Congress, Governors, and State Legislatures.

United Nations Development Program

http://www.undp.org/

UNDP's overarching mission is to help countries build national capacity to achieve sustainable, human development, giving top priority to eliminating poverty and building equity.

The University of Michigan Gerald R. Ford School of Public Policy

http://www.spp.umich.edu/

Formerly the Institute for Public Policy Studies, the Gerald R. Ford School of Public Policy became an independent school within the University of Michigan in 1995. In addition to providing information about the programs offered by the School of Public Policy, the site also provides a working paper archive.

Welfare Policy Center

http://www.hudson.org/wpc/

The Welfare Policy Center (WPC) conducts research and provides technical assistance on welfare reform and related issues. It is a resource for policymakers, program administrators, the press, and many others seeking to learn about cutting-edge welfare reforms and what it takes to make reforms effective. This Web site provides information about key welfare issues and interesting welfare-related articles.

Western New York Law Center

http://www.wnylc.com/web

The Western New York Law Center maintains the Welfare Law Area resource, designed to assist welfare advocates with helpful information.

PREVENTION

Child Abuse Prevention Network

http://child-abuse.com/

Originally developed through an initiative of Family Life Development Center at Cornell University, the network is dedicated to enhancing Internet resources for the prevention of child abuse and neglect, and reducing the negative conditions in the family and the community that lead to child maltreatment.

Committee for Children

`http://www.cfchildren.org/`

Committee for Children provides classroom curricula for the prevention of child abuse and youth violence as well as training and parent education. They also conduct original research evaluating the effectiveness of their programs.

Community Psychology Network

`http://www.cmmtypsych.net/`

Community Psychology Net is the Web's most comprehensive site dedicated to the field of community psychology. This site is meant to be a resource for educators, professionals, researchers, graduate and undergraduate students, and others who are interested in learning more about the fascinating field of community psychology, action research, intervention, and prevention. The site provides links to discussion lists, professional membership groups, graduate schools, course materials, funding sources, position announcements, social policy information, and various other miscellaneous resources relevant to the field.

Let's Prevent Abuse

`http://www.pacer.org/lpa/`

This Minneapolis-based program provides resources to families and professionals for the prevention of child abuse with a focus on disability and cultural competency.

National Clearinghouse on Child Abuse and Neglect Information

`http://nccanch.acf.hhs.gov/`

Supported by the Children's Bureau, The National Clearinghouse on Child Abuse and Neglect Information is a national resource for professionals seeking information on the prevention, identification, and treatment of child abuse and neglect, and related child welfare issues.

Oregon Social Learning Center

`http://www.oslc.org/`

Providing information, educational experiences, and networking opportunities for researchers, interventionists, and advocates dedicated to the science of prevention.

Parents Anonymous

http://www.parentsanonymous.org/

Parents Anonymous is the nation's oldest and largest child abuse prevention organization dedicated to strengthening families through innovative strategies that promote mutual support and parent leadership.

Partnership for a Drug-Free America

http://www.drugfree.org/

This site includes a comprehensive database of drug information: what they do, what they look like, their history, and slang terms.

RESEARCH AND MEASUREMENT

The Action Evaluation Project

http://www.aepro.org/

Action Evaluation is a new method of evaluation, one that focuses on defining, monitoring, and assessing success. Rather than waiting until a project concludes, Action Evaluation supports project leaders, funders, and participants as they collaboratively define and redefine success until it is achieved. Because it is integrated into each step of a program and becomes part of an organization, Action Evaluation can significantly enhance program design, effectiveness and outcome. Participants emerge with a sense that the evaluation process has enhanced and improved program and organizational capacity as they achieve success.

AlphaLogic

http://www.pdq4.com/

Presents the Personality Diagnostic Questionnaire (PDQ-4), a user-friendly interactive program that determines the presence of personality disorders consistent with the DSM-IV, Axis II.

American Evaluation Association

http://www.eval.org/

An international professional association of evaluators devoted to the application and exploration of program evaluation, personnel evaluation, technology, and other forms of evaluation.

American FactFinder

http://factfinder.census.gov/

In 1996, the US Census undertook a comprehensive multi-year development effort to build a data dissemination system. American Fact-Finder uses high performance computing systems to enable users to select data tabulations and maps from data sets in the system.

American Institutes for Research

http://www.air.org/

AIR is an independent, not-for-profit corporation that performs basic and applied research, provides technical support, and conducts analyses in the behavioral and social sciences.

American Psychological Association Science Directorate: Testing and Assessment

http://www.apa.org/science/testing.html

American Psychological Association provides answers to Frequently Asked Questions about the selection and use of psychological tests.

American Sociological Association Section on Methods

http://www.icpsr.umich.edu/methsect/

Provides information about the activities of the section.

ANU—Coombsweb

http://coombs.anu.edu.au/

This archive site was established to act as an electronic repository of the social science and humanities papers, bibliographies, directories, theses abstracts and other high-grade research material produced (or deposited) at the Research Schools of Social Sciences and Pacific and Asian Studies, Australian National University, Canberra, Australia.

Bioethics Resources on the Web

http://www.nih.gov/sigs/bioethics/IRB.html

An excellent list of resources about human subjects research and Institutional Review Boards from the National Institutes for Health.

Bureau of Justice Assistance Evaluation Web Site

http://www.ojp.usdoj.gov/BJA/evaluation/

The Bureau of Justice Assistance is committed to the importance of program evaluation and to developing and enhancing evaluation capabilities at State and local levels. This Web site is designed to provide State Administrative Agency staff, criminal justice planners, researchers and evaluators, as well as local practitioners with a variety of resources for evaluating criminal justice programs.

Buros Institute of Mental Measurements

http://www.unl.edu/buros/

Comprehensive site providing reviews of tests, links to important resources for testing, and standards for utilization of tests.

Campbell Collaboration

http://www.campbellcollaboration.org/

The international Campbell Collaboration (C2) is a non-profit organization that aims to help people make well-informed decisions about the effects of interventions in the social, behavioral and educational arenas. C2's objectives are to prepare, maintain and disseminate systematic reviews of studies of interventions. We acquire and promote access to information about trials of interventions. C2 builds summaries and electronic brochures of reviews and reports of trials for policy makers, practitioners, researchers and the public.

Center for Demography and Ecology

http://www.ssc.wisc.edu/cde/

CDE is a multi-disciplinary faculty research cooperative for social scientific demographic research whose membership includes sociologists, rural sociologists, economists, and historians.

Center for Social Research Methods

http://www.socialresearchmethods.net/

This Web site, developed by Bill Trochim at Cornell, is intended for people involved in applied social research and evaluation. There are many links to other locations on the Web that deal in applied social research methods, previously published and unpublished papers, detailed examples of current research projects, useful tools for researchers (like a guide to selecting a statistical analysis), an extensive online textbook, a bulletin board for discussions, and more.

Cochrane Collaboration

`http://www.cochrane.org`

The Cochrane Collaboration is an international non-profit and independent organization, dedicated to making up-to-date, accurate information about the effects of healthcare readily available worldwide. It produces and disseminates systematic reviews of healthcare interventions and promotes the search for evidence in the form of clinical trials and other studies of interventions. The Cochrane Collaboration was founded in 1993 and named for the British epidemiologist, Archie Cochrane.

Community of Science

`http://www.cos.com/`

The mission of the Community of Science (COS) is to provide rapid, easy-to-use information about scientists and the funding of science. The Community of Science is a global registry designed to provide accurate, timely, easy-to-access information about what new funding opportunities exist, and who is working on what subject, and where.

Content Analysis Resources

`http://www.car.ua.edu/`

Resources to assist researchers utilizing content analysis strategies, including reviews of publications, bibliographies, and software.

ESRC: Economic & Social Research Council

`http://www.regard.ac.uk/ESRCInfoCentre/`

ESRC Society Today is a new Web site offering access to an unrivalled range of high quality social and economic research. It is run by the Economic and Social Research Council (ESRC)—the UK's largest funding agency for research and postgraduate training relating to social and economic issues.

The Foundation Finder

`http://lnp.foundationcenter.org/finder.html`

Foundation Finder allows users to search by grantmaker name—including former, partial, and common names, search by geography to identify grantmakers in a given city, state, or zip code, or search by EIN number. With basic information on more than 86,000 grant-makers in the U.S.—including private foundations, community foundations, grantmaking public charities, and corporate giving programs—Foundation Finder is even more comprehensive than ever before.

Geriatric Depression Scale

http://www.stanford.edu/~yesavage/GDS.html

Scale measuring depression in elderly subjects.

Glossary of Selected Social Science Computing and Social Science Terms

http://odwin.ucsd.edu/glossary/

Covers terms that may be useful in managing data collections and providing basic data services.

Idea Works, Inc.

http://www.ideaworks.com/

An information technology company specializing in the development and publication of expert systems for business, industry, research, and human services. Services include training, consulting, develop-ment, publication, and contract services.

The Illinois Researcher Information Service (IRIS)

http://www.library.uiuc.edu/iris/

The Illinois Researcher Information Service (IRIS) is a unit of the University of Illinois Library at Urbana-Champaign. The IRIS office compiles the IRIS database of funding opportunities. The office also maintains a library of publications (informational brochures, ap-plication guidelines, and annual reports) from over 2,000 funding agencies.

Institute for the Advancement of Social Work Research

http://www.iaswresearch.org/

IASWR was founded in 1993 by five national professional organiza-tions that represent the social work practice and education com-munities. In 2000, a new social work research organization became a sponsor. A freestanding, not-for-profit organization, IASWR serves the research needs of the entire social work profession. Sponsoring organizations are represented on the Board of Directors of IASWR and contribute annually to its financial support. IASWR promotes social work research conducted under the auspices of other academic and professional organizations. IASWR does not conduct or fund social work research directly, except in surveys on behalf of the profession which relate to fulfilling Institute goals.

Institute for Social Research

http://www.isr.umich.edu/

Information about the research facility at the University of Michigan. Includes the Survey Research Center, the Research Center for Group Dynamics, the Population Studies Center, the Center for Political Studies, and the Inter-University Consortium for Political and Social Research.

Internal Validity Tutorial

http://psych.athabascau.ca/html/Validity/

This self-instructional tutorial on internal validity that teaches students to recognize and analyze flaws in the design of clinical experiments.

Internet Resources for Institutional Research

http://airweb.org/links/

Links to assist institutional researchers and faculty and students in higher education in navigating the Internet.

Joanna Briggs Institute

http://www.joannabriggs.edu.au/

The Joanna Briggs Institute is an international Research and Development Unit of Royal Adelaide Hospital established in 1995. The formation of the Institute arose from the recognition of a need for a collaborative approach to the evaluation of evidence derived from a diverse range of sources, including experience, expertise and all forms of rigorous research and the translation, transfer and utilization of the "best available" evidence into health care practice. The Web site is divided into three main areas: the Public Area, which is free access, the Members' Area, which is password restricted, and the Clinical Information and RAPid Databases, which are password restricted. The site contains electronic copies of all Joanna Briggs

Institute collaboration publications including Best Practice Information Sheets, Systematic Reviews and Evaluation Cycle Reports published in the refereed serial Evidence in Health Care Reports, and the Clinical Information Database and associated Practice Manuals.

Mathematica Policy Research, Inc.

http://www.mathematica-mpr.com/

For more than 35 years, Mathematica Policy Research, Inc., has been known for its high-quality, objective research to support decisions about our nation's most pressing social policy problems. The firm has conducted some of the most important studies of health care, welfare, education, employment, nutrition, and early childhood policies and programs in the United States. This research, which crisscrosses the human life span from children's health and welfare to long-term care for elderly people, provides a sound foundation for decisions that affect the well-being of Americans.

National Institutes of Health Funding Opportunities

http://grants.nih.gov/grants/

Information about NIH grant and fellowship programs, applying for a grant or fellowship, policy changes, administrative responsibilities of awardees, the CRISP database, and the numbers and characteristics of awards made by the NIH.

On Being a Scientist: Responsible Conduct in Research

http://www.nap.edu/readingroom/books/obas/

An online publication of the Committee on Science, Engineering, and Public Policy of the National Academy of Sciences.

OpinionMeter

http://www.opinionmeter.com/

Interactive fully-automated polling machine to measure customer satisfaction.

Power Calculator

http://calculators.stat.ucla.edu/powercalc/

Web-based software to determine statistical power.

Psychological Maltreatment of Women Inventory

http://www-personal.umich.edu/~rtolman/pmwimas.htm

Created by Richard Tolman at University of Michigan to investigate woman abuse.

Qualitative Methods (QualPage)

http://www.qualitativeresearch.uga.edu/QualPage/

Resources for qualitative researchers.

RAND

http://www.rand.org/

Through research and analysis, RAND assists public policymakers at all levels, private sector leaders in many industries, and the public at large in efforts to strengthen the nation's economy, maintain its security, and improve its quality of life.

Russell Sage Foundation

http://www.russellsage.org/

The principal American foundation devoted exclusively to research in the social sciences, the Foundation is a research center, a funding source for studies by scholars at other academic and research institutions, and an active member of the nation's social science community.

The SASSI Institute

http://www.sassi.com/

The SASSI Institute is dedicated to providing support to clinicians in their efforts to assess and treat clients with substance-related problems. The Substance Abuse Subtle Screening Inventory (The SASSI) is a brief and easily administered psychological screening measure that helps identify individuals who have a high probability of having a substance use disorder.

Social Science Information Gateway (SOSIG)

http://sosig.esrc.bris.ac.uk/

The Social Science Information Gateway (SOSIG) aims to provide a trusted source of selected, high quality Internet information for researchers and practitioners in the social sciences, business and law. It is part of the UK Resource Discovery Network.

Social Science Research Center

http://www.ssrc.msstate.edu/

The SSRC at Mississippi State University makes available many of their research reports on this site.

Society for Judgment and Decision-Making

http://www.sjdm.org/

The Society for Judgment and Decision Making is an interdisciplinary organization dedicated to the study of normative, descriptive, and prescriptive theories of decision.

StatCenter

http://www.utah.edu/stat/

StatCenter is a set of diverse resources for teaching and learning introductory statistics over the web. It is not a stand-alone course that teaches statistics and delivers credit. It is meant to support teachers and students with already-existing classes.

StatLib

http://lib.stat.cmu.edu/

StatLib is a system for distributing statistical software, datasets, and information by email, FTP, and WWW. It is a service of the Carnegie Mellon University Statistics Department.

Statistical Resources on the Internet

http://www.stat.vt.edu/links.htm

It is provided as a starting point for locating statistics-related information on the World Wide Web.

The Statistics Home Page

http://www.statsoftinc.com/textbook/stathome.html

This Electronic Statistical Textbook offers training in the understanding and application of statistics. The material was developed based on many years of teaching undergraduate and graduate statistics courses and covers a wide variety of applications, including laboratory research, business statistics and forecasting, social science statistics and survey research, data mining, engineering and quality control applications.

University Center for Urban and Social Research

http://www.ucsur.pitt.edu/

Established at University of Pittsburgh to carry out basic and applied social science research, the UCSUR is a focal point for collaborative interdisciplinary and multidisciplinary approaches to social science and policy issues.

Web Resources for Educational Research and Evaluation

http://www.stanford.edu/~davidf/class/
webresources.htm

An excellent set of links, most of which are equally applicable to social work research and evaluation, maintained by David Fetterman.

The World Wide Web Virtual Library: Statistics

http://www.stat.ufl.edu/vlib/statistics.html

A cornucopia of links related to statistics.

SEXUALITY

Coalition for Positive Sexuality

http://www.positive.org/

The Coalition for Positive Sexuality was formed to give teens the information about sexuality they need to take care of themselves and affirm their decisions about sex, sexuality, and reproductive control. They also hope to facilitate dialogue, in and out of the public schools, on condom availability and sex education. Just Say Yes, their irreverent and unabashed comprehensive sex education guide is available here.

Collected Domestic Partner Information

http://www.cs.cmu.edu/afs/cs/user/scotts/
domestic-partners/

A collection of information about the issues of domestic partner policies, same sex marriages, and adoption.

The Data Lounge: Lesbian/Gay Internet

http://www.datalounge.com/

Daily News, Culture and Gossip, Forums and Weekly Surveys. Global Lesbian/Gay Calendar. Web Directory and Edwina's Dating Service.

Deaf Queer Resource Center

http://www.deafqueer.org/

DQRC is a national nonprofit information center. Considered to be "the place" to find comprehensive and accurate information about the deaf queer community.

Gay Canada

http://www.cglbrd.com/

The first GLB community based information network for Canadian gays, lesbians, and bisexuals, this site contains a impressive set of resources, updated frequently.

!OutProud!

http://www.outproud.org/

This the WWW site for the National Coalition for Gay, Lesbian, and Bisexual Youth. The site offers a wide range of resources for youth and educators.

Queer Frontiers

http://www.usc.edu/isd/archives/queerfrontiers/queer/beyond/

1995 Conference Proceedings and Beyond: A Scholarly Resource for Queer Theory and Studies. The focus of ongoing content development for "Beyond 1995" is on a queer theoretically focused investigation, analysis and critique of the Internet's cultural and social significance and impact and how it is itself generating a whole new cyber-culture and subsequent cyber-reality.

Qworld

http://www.qworld.com

Qworld, a "web location for queer information, news, and community," is a fun and informational site hosting two online magazines, chat areas and message boards, a listing of gay-friendly professionals, regional resources, and the Qfiles, which offer everything from health information to shareware.

Transgender Forum

http://www.tgforum.com/

A resource guide for crossdressers, transvestites, transsexuals, trans-gendered people, their family and friends.

Youth Assistance Organization/Youth Action Online

http://www.youth.org

This is a service run by volunteers, created to help self-identifying gay, lesbian, bisexual and questioning youth. YAO exists to provide young people with a safe space online to be themselves. The site offers information for youths questioning their sexuality, an online magazine, and links to other resources on the Internet.

SUBSTANCE ABUSE

Alcoholics Anonymous

http://www.alcoholics-anonymous.org/

Information about the self-help organization.

AL-ANON and ALATEEN

http://www.Al-Anon-Alateen.org/

These are worldwide organizations that offer self-help recovery programs for families and friends of alcoholics whether or not the alcoholic seeks help or even recognizes the existence of a drinking problem.

American Society of Addiction Medicine

http://www.asam.org/

The medical specialty society dedicated to educating physicians and improving the treatment of individuals suffering from alcoholism or other addictions.

AMERSA

http://www.amersa.org/

Association for Medical Education and Research in Substance Abuse, sponsored by the Center for Alcohol and Addiction Studies at Brown University.

APA Division 28

http://www.apa.org/divisions/div28/

American Psychological Association Division 28 is the special interest group for psychopharmacology and Substance Abuse. This page offers their archives and information on research opportunities.

Canadian Centre on Substance Abuse

http://www.ccsa.ca/

A nonprofit organization working to minimize the harm associated with the use of alcohol, tobacco and other drugs, this site offers links to a wealth of resources, including online courses on substance abuse topics.

Center for Alcohol and Addiction Studies

http://www.caas.brown.edu/

Features information about the work of the Brown University center and links to related resources.

Center for Education and Drug Abuse Research

http://cedar.pharmacy.pitt.edu/

Information on CEDAR, an ongoing 20-year prospective family/high-risk study of substance abuse, including grant information, description of the design and research modules, list of publications, news, and links to other drug-related resources.

Center for Substance Abuse Prevention

http://prevention.samhsa.gov/

CSAP Technical Assistance Services to Communities is a unique federally funded program designed to disseminate information, increase dialog, and promote community empowerment to combat alcohol and other drug problems.

Centre for Addiction and Mental Health

http://www.camh.net/

The Centre for Addiction and Mental Health is a public hospital providing direct patient care for people with mental health and addiction problems. The Centre was created in 1998 through the successful merger of the Clarke Institute of Psychiatry, the Addiction Research

Foundation, the Queen Street Mental Health Centre and the Donwood Institute. The Addiction Research Foundation, founded in 1949, was one of North America's pre-eminent facilities for research into alcohol, tobacco and other drug problems. The Foundation's current mission is to work with its partners to create and apply knowledge to prevent and reduce substance abuse in Ontario. The CAMH collaborates with the World Health Organization, participating in international research and carrying out training programs in other countries.

Cocaine Anonymous

http://www.ca.org/

Cocaine Anonymous is a 12-step fellowship of men and women who share their experience, strength and hope with each other so that they may solve their common problem and help others to recover from their addiction.

Dual Diagnosis Web Site

http://users.erols.com/ksciacca/

Dual Diagnosis refers to co-occurring Mental Illness, Drug Addiction and/or Alcoholism in various combinations. This site is designed to provide information and resources for service providers, consumers, and family members who are seeking assistance and/or education in this field.

Harm Reduction Coalition

http://www.harmreduction.org/

The Harm Reduction Coalition (HRC) is committed to reducing drug-related harm among individuals and communities by initiating and promoting local, regional, and national harm reduction education, interventions, and community organizing. HRC fosters alternative models to conventional health and human services and drug treatment; challenges traditional client/provider relationships; and provides resources, educational materials, and support to health professionals and drug users in their communities to address drug-related harm.

LifeRing Secular Recovery

http://www.unhooked.com/

LifeRing is an alternative recovery method for those alcoholics or drug addicts who are uncomfortable with the spiritual content of widely available 12-Step programs.

Narcotics Anonymous

http://na.org/

Narcotics Anonymous is an international, community-based association of recovering drug addicts. Started in 1947, the NA movement is one of the world's oldest and largest of its type, with nearly twenty thousand weekly meetings in seventy countries.

National Alliance of Methadone Advocates

http://www.methadone.org/

NAMA is an organization composed of methadone maintenance patients and supporters of quality methadone maintenance treatment.

National Association of Alcoholism and Drug Abuse Counselors

http://www.naadac.org/

NAADAC's mission is to provide leadership in the alcoholism and drug abuse counseling profession. The site offers information about the organization and links to important resources.

National Organization on Fetal Alcohol Syndrome

http://www.nofas.org/

NOFAS is a nonprofit organization dedicated to eliminating birth defects caused by alcohol consumption during pregnancy and improving the quality of life for those individuals and families affected. NOFAS is the only national organization focusing solely on FAS, the leading known cause of mental retardation.

The New Science of Addiction: Genetics and the Brain

http://learn.genetics.utah.edu/units/addiction/

The Genetic Science Learning Center is an outreach education program located in the midst of bioscience research at the University of Utah. Their mission is to help people understand how genetics affects their lives and society through the development of educational resources which provide accurate and unbiased information about topics in genetics and bioscience. Designed for non-research audiences, our materials are interactive and jargon-free, target multiple learning styles, and often convey concepts through visual elements.

Nicotine and Tobacco Network

http://www.nicnet.org/

NicNet is sponsored by the Arizona Program for Nicotine and Tobacco Research at the University of Arizona. This page is a great place to visit to find resources on quitting and for general information about quitting smoking.

Prevline: National Clearinghouse for Alcohol and Drug Information

http://www.health.org/

Offers electronic access to searchable databases and substance abuse prevention materials that pertain to alcohol, tobacco, and drugs.

The Research Institute on Addictions

http://www.ria.buffalo.edu/

RIA in Buffalo, New York, is a national leader in alcohol and substance abuse prevention, treatment, and policy research. The site offers information about the work of the center, including its Minority Research Development Program.

Sobriety and Recovery Resources

http://www.recoveryresources.org/

Links to personal testimonials and information about self-help, largely 12-step, groups.

Society for Research on Nicotine and Tobacco

http://www.srnt.org/

SRNT is composed of over 500 of the world's leading scientists in tobacco and nicotine research. The mission of the Society is to stimulate the generation of new knowledge concerning nicotine in all its manifestations—from molecular to societal. The site provides links to research resources, training and research opportunities, and other resources.

Substance Abuse and Mental Health Services Administration

http://www.samhsa.gov/

The SAMHSA home page offers links to a wide variety of resources.

VIOLENCE

Act Against Violence Outreach Campaign

http://idahoptv.org/outreach/acts/

Act Against Violence is a multi-year, solutions-based public television outreach effort which combines programming, print materials, and community events to help reduce youth violence.

Bureau of Justice Statistics Crime and Victims Statistics

http://www.ojp.usdoj.gov/bjs/cvict.htm

Information, statistics, and publications about criminal victimization in the United States and related data collections.

Center for the Study and Prevention of Violence

http://www.colorado.edu/cspv/

The Center for the Study and Prevention of Violence (CSPV) was founded in 1992 with a grant from the Carnegie Corporation of New York to provide informed assistance to groups committed to understanding and preventing violence, particularly adolescent violence.

Child Abuse Prevention Network

http://child-abuse.com/

This site is dedicated to using the World Wide Web to give child abuse prevention professionals the fullest possible support in their work. A seemingly inexhaustible reference of links for professionals.

Coalition to Stop Gun Violence

http://www.csgv.org/

The Coalition to Stop Gun Violence was founded to combat the growing gun violence problem in the United States. CSGV is a unique coalition of more than forty religious, professional, labor, medical, educational and civic organizations.

Community United Against Violence

http://www.cuav.org/

CUAV is a 15-year-old nonprofit agency that addresses and prevents hate violence directed at lesbians, gay men, bisexuals, and transgendered persons.

Domestic Violence Handbook

http://www.domesticviolence.org/

This online resource is designed to assist women who are experiencing domestic abuse.

Domestic Violence Hotlines

http://www.feminist.org/911/crisis.html

Links to telephone, postal, and electronic addresses for domestic violence hotlines across the country.

The Family Peace Project

http://www.mcw.edu/display/router.asp?DocID=11599

The Family Peace Project provides education, training and consultation to citizens, health care professionals, organizations and communities. Staff for the Project consists of psychologists and community activists who believe that citizens can improve their communities by using the power of individual responsibility, civic action and the democratic process to engage the strengths and resources of our local communities and create local solutions.

Family Violence Prevention Fund

http://endabuse.org

The Family Violence Prevention Fund works to prevent violence within the home, and in the community, to help those whose lives are devastated by violence. The site provides a host of links to domestic violence sites, allied organizations, and other resources.

Guggenheim Foundation Research on Violence and Aggression

http://www.hfg.org/

The Harry Frank Guggenheim Foundation sponsors scholarly research on problems of violence, aggression, and dominance. The foundation provides both research grants to established scholars and dissertation fellowships to graduate students during the dissertation-writing year. The *HFG Review* of research is published on a semi-annual basis.

The Harvard Youth Violence Prevention Center

http://www.hsph.harvard.edu/hyvpc/

The Harvard Youth Violence Prevention Center (HYVPC) is an innovative, multi-disciplinary center based at the Harvard School of Public Health. The Center's theme is "Research Partnerships with Communities." Center activities are based upon the premise that effective prevention evolves from mutually respectful, reciprocal relationships between researchers, community members, and policy makers.

Justice Information Center (NCJRS): Family Violence

http://www.ncjrs.gov/spotlight/family_violence/
summary.html

A summary of information about family violence, with links to facts and figures, legislation, publications, programs, training and technical assistance, grants and funding, and related resources.

Mapping Policies and Actions

http://www.harbour.sfu.ca/freda/reports/pol.htm

This site presents an annotated bibliography about violence against women. The material in this bibliography is organized into subject areas. The broad subject areas include; criminal justice, civil/family law, health, economic/social welfare, housing, education/curriculum, community-based programs and services and literature reviews.

Minnesota Higher Education Center Against Violence and Abuse

http://www.mincava.umn.edu/

The goal of the Clearinghouse is to provide a quick and user-friendly access point to the extensive electronic resources on the topic of violence and abuse available through the Internet. It offers access to thousands of Gopher servers, interactive discussion groups, newsgroups and Web sites around the world.

The National Center for Victims of Crime

http://www.ncvc.org/

The National Center for Victims of Crime provides assistance to victims of crime and providers of assistance to victims of crime.

National Coalition Against Domestic Violence

http://www.webmerchants.com/ncadv/

NCADV is a grassroots nonprofit membership organization working since 1978 to end violence in the lives of women and children. They provide a national network for state coalitions and local programs serving battered women and their children, public policy at the national level, technical assistance, community awareness campaigns, general information and referrals, and publications on the issue of domestic violence, sponsor of a national conference every two years for battered women and their advocates.

National Consortium on Violence Research

http://www.ncovr.org/

NCOVR has been created as a research and training center devoted to studying the factors contributing to inter-personal violence. The NCOVR World Wide Web site is served by the H. John Heinz III School of Public Policy and Management at Carnegie Mellon University in Pittsburgh, Pennsylvania.

NOW and Violence Against Women

http://now.org/issues/violence

Information from the National Organization for Women about violence against women.

Partnerships Against Violence Network

http://pavnet.org/

PAVNET Online is a "virtual library" of information about violence and youth-at-risk, representing data from seven different federal agencies. It considers itself a "one-stop", searchable, information resource to help reduce redundancy in information management and provide clear and comprehensive access to information for states and local communities.

Rape, Abuse, and Incest National Network

http://www.rainn.org/

RAINN is a nonprofit organization based in Washington, D.C. that operates a national toll-free hotline for victims of sexual assault.

The Silent Witness National Initiative

http://www.silentwitness.net/

In 1990, an ad hoc group of women artists and writers, upset about the growing number of women in Minnesota being murdered by their partners or acquaintances, joined together with several other women's organizations to form Arts Action Against Domestic Violence, which has as its goal the promotion of successful community-based domestic violence reduction efforts in order to reach zero domestic murders by 2010.

Violence Against Women and Sexual Harassment

http://www.feminist.com/violence/

Anti-Violence Resources at Feminist.com.

Violence and Abuse in Couples Project

http://www.ackerman.org/violence.htm

This project has as its goal the development of a feminist-informed, morally explicit systemic conjoint treatment model to end violence by men toward their female partners.

Women, Co-Occurring Disorders & Violence Study

http://www.prainc.com/wcdvs/

The Center for Substance Abuse Treatment, the Center for Substance Abuse Prevention and the Center for Mental Health Services, acknowledging the impact of violence and the role of physical and sexual abuse in the lives of women with serious mental illnesses, have responded by collaborating on the development and administration of this new study. This research is looking at women with alcohol, drug abuse and mental health disorders who have histories of violence. Knowledge that is gained from this multi-site, multi-center study is expected to be useful in advancing national, state and local policy that affects how the various service systems respond to women with co-occurring disorders who have histories of violence, and their children.

MAILING LISTS FOR SOCIAL WORKERS

Child Abuse Prevention Network

http://child-abuse.com/elists.html

Mailing lists for professionals in child abuse prevention and treatment.

Gender-Related Electronic Forums

http://www-unix.umbc.edu/~korenman/wmst/forums.html

Gender-Related Electronic Forums is an annotated, frequently up-dated, award winning listing of publicly accessible electronic forums related to women or to gender issues.

Mental Health Mailing Lists

http://mentalhealth.about.com/library/weekly/aa060297.htm

Mailing lists from About.com.

Psychology and Support Mailing List Pointer

http://psychcentral.com/mail.htm

Alphabetic listing of dozens of support-oriented and professional mailings lists.

Social Work Access Network

http://cosw.sc.edu/swan/listserv.html

One of the most comprehensive listings of social work relevant dis-cussion groups is the Social Work Listservs page maintained by the SWAN. The list references nearly 60 mailing lists related to a variety of aspects of social work practice.

Social Work Resources

http://www.clinicalsocialwork.com/socialwork.html #MAILING

Lists of mailing lists from Pat McClendon, a social work from Louis-ville, Kentucky.

Virtual Social Work Mailing Lists

http://www.socialwork.ndo.co.uk/contacts.htm

Mailing lists from a site devoted to helping British social workers find resources in an Internet environment dominated by the United States.

NOTES

NOTES

NOTES

NOTES